THRIVING

— *in* —

GRACE

Unleashing Wellness
from a Biblical Perspective

KAREN A. DITTMAN
AND MICHAEL G. DITTMAN

Publishing Services provided by Paper Raven Books LLC
Printed in the United States of America
First Printing, 2024

ISBN (Paperback): 979-8-9915132-0-3
ISBN (Hard Cover): 979-8-9915132-1-0

To our mothers, Fran and Jane

See you again soon...

"But blessed is the one who trusts in the Lord,
whose confidence is in him.
They will be like a tree planted by the water
that sends out its roots by the stream.
It does not fear when heat comes;
its leaves are always green.
It has no worries in a year of drought
and never fails to bear fruit."

Jeremiah 17:7-8

CONTENTS

Introduction

"I wish you would stop your rage cleaning and go take care of yourself!" Michael said to me (Karen) one evening, which made my anger boil inside even more.

It all started when I came home after a frustrating afternoon and started venting (okay, complaining) about how our four-year-old was acting. Stressed and overwhelmed with her behavior, I hoped to relieve some of the frustration I was feeling over a child who felt like too much for me to handle on my own. I wanted to be seen. Instead of sympathizing, expressing compassion, or even making random grunts of affirmation, Michael said... nothing. I felt invisible and unimportant. At the time we had a broken dishwasher and a sink piled up with three days' worth of dirty dishes, so I steamed and scrubbed while he dried and wondered why I was so upset. When he tried to encourage me to take a break for some self-care, all I heard was, "You're too much for me right now, so please go away and figure out how to help yourself."

Later that evening, we talked openly about what had happened and came to a better understanding of one another. For me, Michael's response had tapped into unhealthy and toxic messages I had inside since my childhood, including "you're not worth my time." Michael's way of caring for me by standing with me in the moment didn't speak loudly enough to overcome those messages. He was left wondering what he had said that triggered my anger, unaware that his own tendency to shut down when things get hard communicated such difficult things to me.

This type of interaction wasn't frequent, but it also wasn't unusual. We had nearly 34 years of ups and downs, having raised two children to adulthood before suddenly finding ourselves with young children all over again in our 50s. We didn't disagree often, and when we did, we could usually resolve things without an argument. At the time of that "rage cleaning" incident, we were coming out of a season of incredible difficulty that had stressed our family beyond imagining. We were surviving. But there was room for growth, for further opening our hearts. That evening, we took a new step towards Thriving together.

Surviving and Thriving

We see life as a dance between "Survival Mode" and "Thriving." On an average day, many of us are just doing what needs to be done. Sometimes we experience challenges that throw us into Survival Mode. You might find yourself in a relational, financial, mental, emotional, health-related, or other type of crisis, striving to find the way through. This Survival state may last anywhere from hours to years. It is a genuine struggle. However, as you pass through it[1] and find resolution or healing, you can reach a new level of health, a sense of Thriving. We relate this to the Biblical concept of *Shalom*. It's more than simply peace; it's a sense of Wholeness, of being complete as God has done a good work in you (Philippians 1:6).

"Thriving"—this sense of *Shalom*—is the foundation and expression of Biblical Wellness. It looks like peace, rest, resolution that results from facing a struggle and moving through it rather than trying to avoid the pain. Physical strength is developed by pushing muscles to the point of exhaustion so they can grow. In a similar way, spiritual, mental and emotional strength grow out of facing pain and working hand in hand with God to move through the pain towards growth.

Life is a journey of constant growth and transformation. We move in and out of these seasons of Surviving and Thriving as we grow in Wellness. How you respond to the crises that throw you into Survival Mode influences how you move through the difficulties and challenges that you face. Do you blame yourself or God for your struggles, or do you choose to trust that God has a purpose for the pain you endure? Are you aware of your internal self-talk and reactions to the crises you face? How do you engage with others in your life during periods of difficulty—by reaching out or shutting others out? Do you even have a support system? Where do you find the strength you need to get through life's challenges? Do you just "suck it up and get through

---

1: Many Christian authors describe this as "The Wall," an experience of trials that we must endure and pass through in order to grow.

it," or are you able to find strength from God? Your honest answers to these questions may help you recognize whether you're Surviving or Thriving in life right now.

Karen's Story

Several years ago, I was invited into a time of Healing Prayer. Having never experienced this kind of prayer time, and not sure I would gain much from the session, I agreed to give it a try anyway.

"Close your eyes," the leader said. "I want to help you find a safe space inside yourself to go to as needed through this process. Go back to your earliest memory of a time when you felt completely loved and cherished."

"Okay," I thought to myself. "An early memory... feeling loved and cherished. Ummm..."

From that point, I have no memory of the rest of the prayer time. All I remember is being unable to connect with an early memory of feeling that kind of love. It's not that my parents abandoned me or didn't love me. I wasn't abused, and generally, I would have said that I had a happy childhood. However, my mother lived with significant wounds from her childhood, and my father was extremely busy between his work and studying to complete his Bachelor's degree during my earliest years. Yes, they loved me, but I don't remember them taking time to sit and give me the kind of attention that communicated, "You are precious." When I look back now, I see many of my emotional memories of my childhood expressed a search for attention to feel loved.

That moment of realization arrived at a pivotal time in my life. It was also a time when I was struggling with stress, weight gain, parenting challenges, and a heavy burden of guilt over it all. As a homeschooling mom, I found myself feeling burned out for the school year by the end of September and barely limping to the finish by April. I had gained at least 10 pounds the previous winter, and nothing I tried to lose that extra weight worked. I easily lost patience with my children. While I was good at apologizing and admitting my mistakes, I felt tremendous guilt about losing patience to begin with.

All of this—the stress, the weight gain, and the frustrations of parenting—had me utterly exhausted. I wanted to exercise regularly, knowing that it would help with my stress and long-term health, but I was so sedentary that I could barely get out of the house once a week to walk with my friends. Even more, I battled depression and longed to find peace and joy in my life. Something had to change. If I didn't find some help in discovering and addressing the root of my brokenness, I risked damaging my relationship with my children while facing decades of growing unhappiness and hopelessness and potentially developing significant health struggles that run in my family.

So I reached out to a friend who had been offering me help for a while. That moment—when I decided to ask for help in my spiritual and emotional journey—changed everything. It was the first of a few shifts I made that helped me move towards greater spiritual, physical, mental, and emotional health. I had to face pain and endure struggles, but I had reached the point where the pain of staying the same was greater than the pain of changing.

Fast forward three or four years. I had newfound energy and physical fitness—not only was I exercising regularly, but I had become a fitness instructor. A surprise third child had come along, and I had new resources to parent her as well as our two teens. I found tools to deal with my stress in a healthy way. Even more importantly, like my friend, I had gone on to serve other women and help them achieve spiritual transformations.

Michael's Story (in his own words)

Michael has his own story of finding healing. In his case, it took a good bit of time to discover the roots of his pain rather than a moment of realization like Karen experienced.

"In the two years before we moved to Colorado, two of my lifelong dreams—to be a father and to be a pastor—were ripped away. First, my immune system was diagnosed as being the incurable cause of our infertility. And then I was asked to step down after only a few months as a first-time pastor, given no opportunity to grow and learn from my mistakes. Karen and I were both deeply wounded and depressed and hoped for healing. In his faithfulness, God led us through that period of grief and gave us a new home, including a wonderful church family. Our visible wounds healed, and we became functional again. We re-engaged in ministry, pouring ourselves out for others. We grieved our infertility and eventually decided we had love to spare. We adopted first a son and then, 20 months later, his biological sister. We joined a church plant. We taught. We served. We loved. We led.

"But the deep wounds were still there, and then physical pain started. One day, with no apparent trigger, I began to experience severe inflammation and stiffness that settled into all my joints. For a decade, I was in nearly constant, often debilitating pain. Sometimes it was mild, and I could function. Other times, it felt like someone was pounding on my joints with a hammer, and I could barely walk or even sit upright. Doctors found no cause for it. I was prescribed increasingly dangerous drugs that did nothing to help and in one case caused a terrible allergic reaction. Even though I am extremely skeptical of most 'alternative' wellness approaches, I tried a highly recommended natural solution that ended up causing even more unpleasant reactions. All anyone could tell me was that I appeared to have an autoimmune condition.

"Slowly, I sank into a functional despair. My wife was suffering and needed me. Our children needed me. My work needed me. Our church needed me. So I coped. I survived. But the pain changed me. I sank into myself. I lost joy. I clung to a sliver of hope, showed up when I had to, and did what was needed. But I suffered. Night after night, I prayed for relief. Day after day, I clung to the only thing I knew for sure, that God is good, and that He loves me. And so I hung on.

"Over time, I began to observe patterns in my symptoms. I slowly identified a number of dietary triggers and environmental factors that triggered or increased my pain. Three years of slow experimenting led to gradual healing. Finally after 13 years, a deep dietary cleanse gave my damaged immune system a reboot. Not only did the pain disappear, but Karen became pregnant. We learned two weeks before our twenty-fifth anniversary that our biological miracle baby was on the way! Now I am stronger, healthier, and happier in my late fifties than I was in my thirties."

In all of this, neither of us feel like we have "arrived" or reached the pinnacle of Wellness. However, we are growing and have tools to help us. The lessons and tools we both learned were the keys to moving past being a stressed-out, overwhelmed, fatigued, unhealthy woman and a pain-ridden man gradually losing hope for restoration. These tools are helping us become the healthy people we are today, and they form the basis of this book you are holding right now.

Our World's Struggle with Pursuing Wellness

Living in a post-pandemic world, we look back on everything that has happened since early 2020 and ask ourselves why things went the way they did. Since the beginning of COVID-era quarantines, we have seen steep rises in depression, anxiety, drug and alcohol abuse, overdose deaths, and suicide/suicidal ideation. At the same time, prescription drugs to treat mental health have become less available.[2] Obesity in the US remains at an all-time high, with 41.9 percent of Americans falling into this category.[3] Americans' trust in our government *and* one another has been steadily declining.[4] Are all of these troubles

---

2: Panchal, Nirmita, et al. "The Implications of COVID-19 for Mental Health and Substance Use." *KFF.Org*, KFF, 20 Mar. 2023, www.kff.org/mental-health/issue-brief/the-implications-of-covid-19-for-mental-health-and-substance-use/.
3: Farberman, Rhea. "State of Obesity 2023: Better Policies for a Healthier America." *TFAH*, Trust for America's Health, 21 Sept. 2023, www.tfah.org/report-details/state-of-obesity-2023/.
4: Newport, Frank. "Americans' Trust in Themselves." *Gallup.Com*, Gallup, 8 Oct. 2021, news.gallup.com/opinion/polling-matters/355553/americans-trust-themselves.aspx.

the result of the COVID pandemic—or were there underlying issues that the stress of the pandemic brought to light? We tend to believe that the latter is true. Before 2020, most of us felt generally okay. But unprecedented lockdowns, shortages, and disruptions to our lives brought many people to a point where they couldn't hold things together anymore. It was all too much, and isolation from one another made everything worse. COVID was the proverbial "straw that broke the camel's back." Granted, it was much larger than a "straw," but as a whole we were already burdened to near breaking.

Even in our own stories, we see hints of reaching a breaking point in our lives. For Karen, the night in Healing Prayer brought to the surface some deep wounds that she could no longer keep buried. While Michael's physical pain seemed to appear out of nowhere, the reality is that his body had been carrying the effects of foods that had been slowly amping up his immune system until it turned on his body. Rather than being a symptom of disease, his pain was an alarm bell, a warning that he needed to make significant changes in his diet.

The people we talk with are dealing with similar struggles. You might suffer, like Michael did, with health issues that doctors don't know how to address looking at the research available to them. Or maybe you find yourself overwhelmed with stress and don't know how to manage it well. Perhaps you struggle with sleep and insomnia, resulting in feeling sluggish and unproductive. Taking expensive supplements has become a popular recommendation, but how can you know you're taking what your body needs? In all of this, you may wrestle with finding time for God and engaging people who support and encourage you. And exercise? It's a challenge to find time for that, too.

Very few people live lives free of stress. Working hard, physical and emotional pain, unhealthy relationship patterns, and failing to take time to resource our souls in God all add up. Looking around at others living this way, you've probably convinced yourself that your life is normal and that you're doing just fine. But are you truly satisfied with a life that is "just fine," a life in Survival Mode? Or do you crave more? This book will show you the simple but not always evident concepts that we learned to Thrive, to live in growing Wellness.

An Unexpected Path to Wellness

If you have become aware that your life is unbalanced or unwell in some way, it's likely you have been looking for a program or formula so you can get fixed and move on. Perhaps you see physical, mental, emotional, and spiritual "health" as their own problems. That can lead you to ask what has worked for others and then try to make their solutions work for you. There are plenty of gurus offering their prescriptions, and friends are always filled with advice based on what has worked for them. But if you fail to achieve the results you're seeking, you probably blame yourself. This has become an epidemic of failure for far too many people. This formulaic approach just doesn't work because every person is uniquely different. What works for one person doesn't necessarily work for another. In addition, most "wellness" programs focus solely on nutrition and exercise while neglecting other parts of the self, including areas that, when out of balance, increase stress and sabotage progress towards health.

But remember our stories. When Karen reached out to a friend, her friend offered the support of an intensive Christ-focused retreat weekend that she had served with for many years. The beauty of this weekend—and what started Karen's journey to spiritual and emotional healing—was that it offered *individualized* support. Karen learned to seek God and what he says to her about herself and her life, and she began to look inside herself for the resources needed for transformation. Step by step, hand in hand with God, she began to make small, simple decisions that led to powerful change. In Michael's case, steps that worked for others such as medical treatment or alternative medicine didn't help at all. Instead, he identified simple but profound diet changes that restored him to health. Michael approaches his struggles with a scientifically curious but skeptical approach rather than an attitude of "I'll try anything as long as it isn't harmful," while Karen takes a more open approach to physical issues. Both are in line with our own perspectives and are perfectly appropriate for each of us.

As much as we'd like to have a one-size-fits-all solution to individual growth and transformation, none exists. As a unique individual, you need to seek direction from God, who created you individually and knows you intimately. Someone else's prescribed program may or may not work for you. It's far more likely that you will spend money on multiple programs looking for the one that fits you. We offer a very different approach. In this book, we will introduce you to the tools of Curiosity, Connection, and Grace. Using these simple tools, you can begin to experience more freedom and joy in life by exploring what is best for you rather than enduring the pressure of following someone else's system. We invite you to become aware of what works and doesn't work for your unique self. We'll encourage you to improve your connections to God, others, and yourself. Finally, tapping into God's Grace to move forward, you can Thrive in your life.

Our goal in this book is to offer you tips and suggestions that are practical without being prescriptive. We recognize you as an individual with unique needs and responses, and we want to help you step into your role as the expert on yourself and what makes you Thrive. Therefore, what works for you may or may not align with what works for anyone else. And that's okay. In fact it's not just okay—it's actually normal!

When Michael and I stopped looking outside ourselves for the solutions to our struggles and instead began asking God and ourselves for the solutions, things changed. We changed. We began to Thrive. The circumstances of our lives didn't shift much, and we still lived under high stress. Yet we learned to embrace gratitude for things as they were, to trust what God was doing, and to look with hope towards the future. This has led us to Thrive in many areas of our lives.

While we are still learning and growing, we offer you this book. We have based our teachings about Wellness on what God says in the Bible. We begin with Curiosity about ourselves and seek Connection with God and others. Transformation does not happen in isolation, nor is it something we will fully achieve in this life. But we want to reassure you that it can happen. Simple shifts in mindset and action, informed by Curiosity and Connection and empowered by God's Grace, can lead to lifelong change. You *can* live a full, abundant life in Christ. Choosing to take even one step in a new direction will put you on a completely different path. Later, we hope you will be able to look back to this moment in your life as one small change that dramatically altered your future.

What Lies Ahead

Over the next nine chapters, we will outline a path of growth into Wellness from a Biblical perspective. We recognize that this is a lifelong pursuit that none of us will achieve fully in life. However, growth and transformation are possible, leading to greater freedom, joy, and peace.

With that in mind, in the first part we will begin by explaining a Biblical approach to Wellness. It starts with understanding that before you can be filled and renewed, you may need to be emptied of what lies in the way of change. The concept of *bara*, or being emptied in order to be filled, is essential to a healthy connection with God in the transformation process. From there, we'll explain what we mean by Curiosity and Connection. We will demonstrate how God's Grace infuses and empowers the transformative process. The second part of this book lays out seven areas of Wellness. We have divided these up into two areas. The "Core Four" make up what we generally think of as self: our Physical, Spiritual, Mental, and Emotional parts. The "Connection Three" involve how we relate to God and the world around us. These include Relational, Vocational, and Financial Wellness. In each of these seven areas, we will share Biblical truths followed by some practical suggestions for growth and questions to explore to help you identify where you may be blocked from growth.

Finally, we will conclude with a few more guiding principles for you to practice as you move forward. We will offer insights into the process of transformation, exploring how moving towards growth in one area can bring change in your life as a whole. We will offer some insights into Self-Care along with a new model that we call Mutual

Care. And we'll conclude with a deeper understanding of *Shalom* as the Wellness and Wholeness that we aim for in our lives.

While we won't offer a specific system or formula to follow in order to achieve growth in these areas, we will share a simple but profound path to transformation in life. We offer you what we have learned from our personal experiences and from working with others. While our teachings are based on the Bible, we don't expect that everyone who comes to this book believes as we do. However, if you are open to the Bible's teachings as a guide for life, you will find a great deal of help in this book.

Overall, we encourage you to pursue your own path to growth. Don't worry whether it looks like ours or anyone else's. Your path will be unique to you. This is a road we have walked and continue to walk, and we invite you on the journey with us.

For Further Study

We have created a Reflection Journal you can download here: http://thrivingjournal.1fit-wellness.com

This journal is designed to help you note your thoughts as you read through the book. You might also want to purchase the Bible study guide we wrote to go along with this book. The study, *Bringing Grace Home*, is set up for you to do deeper individual study and then participate in a small-group discussion once a week for ten weeks.

Authors' Notes

On using our voices: As we worked together on this book, we each brought our own strengths to the project. In one sense, it is difficult to say where Karen's or Michael's "words" are on the pages you're about to read. As a diligent student and teacher of the Bible who loves to dig into everything God has to say on any given subject, Michael did the bulk of the background study and synthesis that forms the Biblical basis of this book. Karen put nearly all of the words on paper. For that reason, the voice in this book will alternate between "we" and "I." To avoid the awkwardness of needing to specify Karen as the speaker when telling a personal story, anything stated in the first person "I" is her words (with the exception of Michael's story told in his own words above in the introduction).

Regarding the stories and case studies: The stories used throughout this book are from real people who have shared their lives and experiences with us. Names have been changed to protect their privacy. Case studies in Part 2 of this book are composites of multiple stories and experiences. We use these case studies to illustrate how the principles we teach may play out in real-life situations.

Part One

A Biblical Approach
to Wellness

CHAPTER 1

Bara: Empty to be Filled

"I went away full, but the LORD has brought me back empty."

Ruth 1:21a

"In the beginning, God *created* the heavens and the earth" (Genesis 1:1, emphasis added). The most significant and foundational principle of our teaching is this: God made everything that exists. Including *you*. God had an intention and design from the beginning of time for the entire universe, from the smallest microorganism to the brightest star. God made you with purpose and intention. He created your body, your soul, your mind, and your heart. He brought you to this planet at the time and place he designed for a very real purpose. If you hear nothing else, if you stop reading after this paragraph, please remember this truth: you matter, and you matter here and now!

With that in mind, let's take a closer look at the word "created" because it's essential to where we need to go from here.[5] The Hebrew word is *bara*, and it follows an interesting thread throughout scripture. The same word is used in Joshua 17:15 where Joshua tells descendants of Joseph that if they don't have enough land because their families are growing, they should go into the forest and "clear land" for themselves. They needed to create space for their tribe in the same way that God created the earth in the beginning.

The same word is used in Isaiah 45:18:

For this is what the Lord says—
He who created the heavens, he is God;
He who fashioned and made the earth,
He founded it;
He did not create [*bara*] it to be empty, but formed it to be inhabited.

When God made the earth, the whole universe in fact, it was empty, filled with nothing. But God intended for it to be filled with all he was about to make. We can adopt this same perspective in our own lives. As you seek to make changes (following God's leading), you may find that you need to empty yourself of things that are not good, not in line with what he wants for you or what his word teaches. But we never empty ourselves simply for the sake of being empty. God intends to fill us with what is good and healthy!

How do we know what is good and healthy—what we are meant to fill our lives with? First, learn what God says is good. The

_____

5: For a more in-depth look at this, see Gene Binder's sermon at Cornerstone Church of Boulder Valley, Oct 14, 2015, here: https://youtu.be/gKb-JQzZBXk

Scriptures form the basis of the second part of this book where we outline a model for wellness in each of seven areas. Admittedly, we can learn from science, including psychology, biology, chemistry, sociology, environmental sciences, and more. Ultimately, however, God who created the world has the first and last word. Amazingly, more and more, the sciences are discovering details about how our brains and bodies work that are in alignment with teachings in the Bible. For example, neuroscience has discovered that our brains don't distinguish between something we're actually experiencing or something that we're thinking about.[6] This lends an even deeper understanding of Jesus's teachings in Matthew 5:21-28. Wishing harm on another person in anger is no different in your brain than causing harm to that person. Indulging in lust or imagining an illicit relationship is not different than actually committing adultery.

We need to rely on what God says throughout the Bible to learn what is good for us. Notice we don't say what is "right" or "perfect" or "best." We seek to live in Goodness, not perfection, because perfection is God's alone. One day when we meet Jesus face to face, he promises to make us perfect as he is perfect. But in this life, we aim for growth in what God calls "good."

This idea of "Goodness" is like the satellite that provides data to the GPS of our lives.[7] Have you ever tried to follow a GPS route

---

6: Hamilton, David. "Does Your Brain Distinguish Real from Imaginary?" *David R Hamilton, PhD*, 9 Aug. 2022, drdavidhamilton.com/does-your-brain-distinguish-real-from-imaginary/.

7: Pursuing "Goodness" in life is pursuing a return to the ideal world God created. In Genesis 1, God repeatedly said "it is good." We are aware that we cannot return to this state of perfection in a fallen world, yet we can seek as much as possible to live a life that reflects God's intention while living in hope of that full restoration God has promised (Revelation 21).

that was out of sync with reality? Sometimes it can cause frustration and delays, such as getting caught in traffic held up by construction. Sometimes it can be downright dangerous. We once followed our GPS on what appeared to be the most direct route, but it actually took us down a narrow rural dirt road with potential to damage our car. We follow what God teaches us in the Bible because that will not lead us astray. If we believe that God created each of us and placed us at a specific time and place in the history of the world, then what sense does it make to try to follow our own reasoning—or even worse, the logic of a world that denies God? Instead, let's sync the GPS of our lives to follow the routes God has created.

It is not our desire in this book to point fingers at any lifestyles or choices and call them out as "sinful," "ungodly," or "not God's will." We honor you as a person who is able to read the Bible and see what it has to say about your actions and choices. You can pay attention to the voice of the Holy Spirit. The institution of the Church in America has spent too much energy attempting to convict others for perceived sins. As a result, far too many people who are loved and treasured by God have been subjected to humiliation, dehumanization, and alienation. In this book, we desire to turn away from that ugliness and let God convict others where he sees fit. We can only take responsibility for ourselves and our growth as God leads us. We encourage you to continually seek God's direction in your life as you seek to grow in Wellness.

Jesus said in John 10:10 that he came "that [you] might have life, and have it to the full." Living in alignment with the guiding principles of God's Word, you can move towards the full, abundant, healthy, overflowing life that Jesus said he came to give! Allow God to fill your life with the Good he intends for you.

One beautiful way to practice *bara* is through gratitude. Many influencers in recent years have begun encouraging us to practice gratitude by writing down gratitude lists, adding three to 10 new items each day to the list. This is a great beginning, and we don't want to discount the value of becoming aware of the good things that God is doing in, around, and through you by listing them and reflecting on them.

However, we see gratitude as a deeper practice. We can thank God not just *in* but also *for* every circumstance (see 1 Thessalonians 5:16-18 and Hebrews 13:15) because he is good and loving. This applies even when God orchestrates or allows circumstances that are really, really hard. Through gratitude, you empty yourself of your own expectations and allow God to fill you with his love and goodness.[8] You can release to him the burdens you don't need to carry, allowing him to take them on, and choose to take up faith and trust in what he is doing. Ultimately, gratitude becomes much more than simply saying "thanks." It leads to a deep, abiding, trusting relationship with God. This happens largely through emptying yourself of things that block you from true gratitude and creating space for the Holy Spirit to fill.

As you continue through this book, let the Holy Spirit speak to you. Ask God to show you what areas of your life are not fully aligned with his GPS of what is "Good" and what he wants for you. There is no condemnation for you here (Romans 8:1). Don't judge yourself when God reveals an area of your life that is out of alignment with what he wants for you. We invite you simply to explore what you need to let go of (emptying yourself) and seek what God will give you in

---

8: For a helpful guide to learn to practice this kind of gratitude in your life, check out our journal *The Fruit of Gratitude* available through Amazon: https://a.co/d/h2WWwIY

return. He longs to fill you with his love and Goodness. The process of becoming transformed into the person God means you to be may be challenging. *But* it is worth it! Speaking of this work that God is doing in his children, Paul wrote in Romans 8:18-19, "I consider that our present sufferings are not worth comparing with the glory that will be revealed in us. For the creation waits in eager expectation for the children of God to be revealed." All of creation is just waiting to see who God is making you to be, and we are excited to be on this journey with you.

CHAPTER 2

Curiosity: The Simple Power of Awareness

"It is the glory of God to conceal a matter;
to search out a matter is the glory of kings."

Proverbs 25:2

Several years ago, I was looking for a new exercise routine that I could do at home. I had been trying a number of different things, but I wanted to find something that wouldn't take a lot of time, didn't call for special equipment, and didn't require doing burpees. I had a conversation with my cousin who was familiar with a variety of exercise formats, and she suggested I try PiYO, a format that I had never experienced. The video series challenged me in ways that no exercise program ever had. Stretched both literally and figuratively as I learned to do new movements based on Pilates and Yoga, I gradually grew stronger and more flexible. The exercise program was fun and rewarding, and motivated me to dive into other strength training. Before long, I found myself in the most physically fit state I had been in for over two decades. I took a leap into what had been a back-burner "impossible dream" of teaching fitness classes when I trained to be a PiYO LIVE instructor. But it all started with Curiosity. When I tried something new and discovered how much I loved it, I learned the power of an "Aha Moment" revelation.

I've had the same experience many other times, sometimes (unfortunately) in reverse. After following a gluten-free diet for a few years, I went on a short-term mission trip. During that trip, I chose to let go of the gluten-free diet for a couple of weeks, instead of asking the people preparing food to accommodate my restrictions. Mostly, I was okay because it wasn't hard to avoid the wheat-based foods in my meals. But after having pizza for dinner one night, the next day, I was exhausted. It didn't take me long to associate how I felt with what I had eaten, and that "Aha Moment" led me to be far more diligent about my food choices from then on. Sometimes the "Aha" comes in a moment of realization. Sometimes, as Michael experienced in his healing process, it takes significant time and a lot of exploration.

The "Aha Moment" forms the foundation of the principle of Curiosity that we believe is crucial to Wellness. Every person—body, heart, mind, and spirit—is uniquely made and will respond differently to food, exercise, or other choices or experiences. As a very basic example, women are different from men—different hormones and muscle structure mean diet and exercise plans will bring different results. Age makes a difference, too. We all know this. Other factors such as genetic predispositions, gut biome composition, and cultural factors influence our individual responses. As an example of genetic factors, we learned when our daughter was three years old that she has a genetic predisposition to a host of autoimmune diseases ranging from Celiac Disease to Type 1 Diabetes to Lupus—genes that are "activated" by gluten in the diet. As a result, her doctor prescribed a completely gluten-free diet for life. Even before her doctor recommended the testing, we had already intuitively known it was a problem because of our own observations. Since both of us have issues with gluten, we had kept her from eating anything with wheat for more than a year in her life. After I introduced it into her diet, I began noticing unusual skin reactions that went away when I took it out. Ultimately, my observations combined with family history led to seeking a medical diagnosis.

This doesn't only apply to Physical Wellness, though. Later in this book, we'll dive more deeply into exploring the different areas of our lives, but for now, we can look at how this "Aha Moment" shows up in other ways. You can use Curiosity to identify thought processes that are impacting your Mental Wellness. The stories you tell yourself about your experiences in life become more important than the experiences themselves. Erika, for example, has a history of trauma in her relationships with men. Recently in talking about her internship for a new career, she commented, "Why do these boys always want something from me?" Aha! That simple comment led to a realization of deeper places she needed to look into that were impacting how she had been showing up in her interactions with her coworkers. As she continues to process how her emotional wounds have impacted her, she is growing towards more health and Wellness in her relationships. Erika's story shows how identifying the story through Curiosity and an "Aha Moment" becomes the basis for transformation.

That's the power of Curiosity. Just taking time to be aware of how a particular habit, food, exercise, mental story, or relationship impacts you can lead you to making a more appropriate choice, whether or not it's what "experts" and "professionals" recommend. Here are some other examples:

- Experts recommend exercising in the morning, or at least in the first part of your day, because exercising in the evening may raise cortisol levels and make sleep harder. So try it. But if the kind of exercise you prefer makes you too tired to function for the rest of the day, maybe try the evening and see if it helps you sleep better.

- Christians are expected to have a daily "Quiet Time" of Bible reading and prayer. Again, we're usually told to spend that time with God in the morning before starting the day. But what if your mornings are too chaotic? Once you get into your day, do you feel like it's too late and you've messed everything up? Then by the end of the day when things have quieted down, maybe you can't stay awake to read and pray. So what does a healthy connection to God look like for you? Using Curiosity to find what is right for you in your season of life could lead to something unexpected like a midafternoon meditation, listening to scripture through an audio app during your commute, or random moments of gratitude and prayer throughout your day (possibly with alarms on your phone as reminders) as opposed to a prescribed way of spending time with God.

- If you have struggled with depression or anxiety, surely you've heard the message "Joy is a choice. Christians shouldn't need medication." (Fortunately, most thinking along these lines is less common than it used to be, but it still exists.) We will address the area of Mental Wellness more specifically later in the book. Still, using this principle of Curiosity, you might explore how meditation or music might help. Are there certain times of day, seasons of the year, events, or people who trigger the tendency to go "down?" What helps you come out of it? When you become aware of what might lie beneath your struggles, you can use that awareness to help you make a plan for managing them. This is not to say that medication is not the answer—it might be, and that is worth exploring on your own instead of following the expectations of others.

Curiosity requires slowing down and paying attention. Some tools that can help you begin to make these connections might include journaling, a food log, or phone apps that track activity and sleep. These tools can help you begin to connect what you do and who you spend time with to how you feel. Do certain foods leave you feeling tired? Does your daily activity impact your sleep? Does your sleep quality impact your mental and emotional well-being and relationships? Which thoughts, stories, or people in your life help you, and which ones seem to make things worse?

I often tell participants in my fitness classes to pay attention to how they feel in the moment as they exercise, reminding them that "you are the one who has to live in your body, not me." I'm aware that as the "professional" in the front of the room, I can offer guidance, but I can't know how another person experiences the exercises I lead. In the same way, *you* are the one who experiences the benefits or consequences of your choices in any area of your life. So as you choose changes or shifts for your life, pay attention to what you experience as a result. Happiness or stress? Pain or relief? Deeper connection to God and others or more distance? Restless nights or better sleep? If something is hard, ask yourself what about it is difficult or challenging—is it tapping into difficult parts of your story, or is it just so different that change feels impossible?

Remember that—other than God—you are the only expert on yourself. Other professionals are experts in their fields based on broad, general knowledge, and research. But no one else has to live as you. At the same time, be aware that some prescriptions and programs are designed to treat and mask symptoms, not to uncover and deal with root issues. The diet and weight-loss industry is notorious for treating obesity as a problem with food consumption or metabolism alone. But what if a person's weight gain is due to an imbalanced gut biome or deeply rooted beliefs of unworthiness? No calorie restriction, macro tracking, or specific weight-loss plan will correct these issues. (And so we have a world full of yo-yo dieters.) But when you become Curious about yourself and begin to explore what works—and doesn't work—for you as an individual, you can make progress in areas where you may have been stuck for years.

Perhaps this concept is new to you. Maybe looking inside feels uncomfortable. That's okay. Take one small step at a time. You might simply stop at set times throughout the day to pay attention to what you're thinking and feeling. After that feels a little more comfortable, then take an extra moment to ask yourself why you may be thinking and feeling that way. Slowly build this habit of Curiosity into your life, and you will begin to experience those helpful "Aha Moments."

As we go through each area of Wellness later in the book, we will suggest tools to help you engage your own Curiosity and help you grow in each of the seven areas of Wellness. For now, simply understand the underlying principle. You are a unique individual. You live with yourself every moment of every day, and you know yourself better than anyone else except God. Let that knowledge work for you!

CHAPTER 3

Connection: The Restoring Power of True "Fitness"

"It takes a grinding wheel to sharpen a blade, and so one person sharpens the character of another."

Proverbs 27:17 TPT

Curiosity is essential to begin your journey towards Wellness, as you become aware of what might need to change and how specific changes affect you. Connection is the next step along the path. You need to build Connection to God, to others, and to yourself. We will look at each of these in reverse order.

Rosa has lived her life disconnected from herself. She often followed her impulses rather than carefully considering her actions and their consequences. She began to lose touch with what she really wanted, so she let others make choices for her to the point where she lost her ability to make choices at all. She let her life be dominated by others, and some of these people abused her trust in traumatic and damaging ways. Over time, she fell into numbing behaviors so she wouldn't have to feel her emotions (negative or positive), believing it was better to feel nothing than to have to feel the grief of loss and the pain of how others had hurt her. Ultimately, she lost touch with herself as a human and fell into destructive addictions.

Rosa's story is an extreme example of what can happen when a person is not Connected to her self. Without Connection to your self, Curiosity is impossible—you cannot be aware of what might or might not be a healthy choice or whether your choices are helpful or hurtful. At the same time, Connection to self begins with Curious awareness of who I am and what I need. Am I hungry or satisfied? Am I tired or rested? What emotions am I experiencing in this moment? Am I sad? Angry? Resentful? What do I desire? Am I satisfied with my life and work? What are the good things in my life right now, and what would I like to see change? Identifying these things is the first step to determining what to do to see change.

Most of us tend to go through our days either on autopilot or just letting things happen to us and around us without slowing down to ask questions like these. That "status quo" is generally fine. Yet it's important to take time to become aware and Connected. As an example of this, I have had to learn when I feel strong emotions to stop and ask myself what is under that emotion—what I really want or need, or what from my past might be triggering that emotional reaction. When I do so, I can stop a destructive outburst before it happens—but when I don't, I might lash out at another person or turn my frustration inward and harm myself (which for me can look like negative self-talk or emotional eating). Neither is acceptable!

Besides Connection with your self, you need Connection with others. We all need community—people in our lives who will help us grow and become more like Christ. A healthy community will see all members growing in Wellness, even if it's in different areas of life. There's a fairly well-known saying that you will become the sum of the five people you spend the most time with. This perspective is supported by what neuroscientists call "mirror neurons." We have neural pathways in our brains that reflect what we experience in relationships with others.[9] For better or worse, our brains are wired to become more like the people we spend time with. This plays out in two ways: experiencing empathy and growing more like those in our communities.

Who makes up a community? It may be your faith community or a small group. It may be the people you work with, your family, or a group of friends who meet together regularly. Or maybe you're part of a group that serves together. Consider the people you spend more time with than others. Who do you think of as "your people?" That's your community. Be careful, however, not to limit your community solely to people you get along with easily. Growth in community often requires bumping up against one another in uncomfortable ways. Conflicts can be helpful when people learn to listen to one another and resolve differences. Emotions such as anger, disappointment, and frustration that arise in relationships can point to a part of your heart that needs healing or growth. Community groups that are characterized by being happy and never disagreeing could be groups that are stagnant and not experiencing true Connection.

9: To see this in action, watch https://www.youtube.com/watch?v=5Th0aOoX4EM. Pay special attention to your own response around 5:30 to 7:00 minutes in the video.

We want to address a common argument that if Jesus spent his time with sinners, then as his followers, we should do the same, seeking to lead them to him. Can we stop for a moment and acknowledge that since Jesus was God incarnate, his brain could never be swayed by others? We're not saying that there is no place for relationships with people who don't share our beliefs. However, Paul also wrote, "Do not be deceived: bad company corrupts good character" (1 Corinthians 15:33). It's important to balance relationships with people we want to influence for good with relationships with people who will help us grow closer to Jesus. In doing so, prioritize the relationships and community that support your growth into Wellness.

Take a moment to evaluate your community—the people you spend the most time with—around the principles we set out. Do you have people in your life who are seeking to grow closer to Jesus, who are growing in one or more areas of Wellness, who are modeling healthy Connections to self, others, and God? Do you know people who are thriving in one or more of the seven areas we will discuss later? If so, then seek them out and spend more time with them! If not, then do you know people who would be open to growing in these areas—you might invite them to do a study together of this book using our guide *Bringing Grace Home*. If you're at a total loss, reach out to us for ways you can connect with the 1Fit Wellness community of people who are seeking to grow in these areas.

Finally—and of foremost importance—seek Connection with God. It makes sense that you know yourself better than others know you, yet God knows you even better. He made you, and he has a plan, purpose, and intention for your life. When you can remain in Connection with God through the Holy Spirit, then you can seek wise direction in your choices. Through prayer and listening to God's voice, you can move towards Wellness and Thriving in life.

However, with all of that said, you may struggle to feel truly Connected in your relationship with God. Gracelynn shared with me that she has a hard time praying or experiencing God in any real way. She grew up with a single mom who was struggling to make ends meet, and one of her siblings had been sucked into addiction. Gracelynn and her mom were both intent on rescuing her sibling. With the kind of drama, chaos, and even trauma Gracelynn experienced in her early adolescent and teen years, it's not surprising that she struggles to trust God. Life's circumstances taught her that she couldn't trust anyone and that she needed to stay vigilant and in control of everything. But prayer requires trust and releasing the outcome to God! If life has taught you that when you're not in control bad things will happen to yourself or the people you love, then that healthy Connection with God may not form properly. For that matter, living with trauma and feeling like life is out of control can prevent healthy Connection from forming with others and even yourself.

So if you see yourself in this sense of dis-Connection from God and others, there is still hope, even if you've experienced trauma[10] in your life. For Gracelynn—and for countless others—admitting the struggle was the first step to building a new trust and Connection with God. God longs for us to turn to him in trust, and he can restore what has been broken. Consider what he says in Isaiah 44:22-23:

10: Traumatic experiences are unique to each individual. Do not minimize your own experience because "it's not as bad as someone else had it." Trauma is a legitimate response to any distressing experience. For more, see https://www.camh.ca/en/health-info/mental-illness-and-addiction-index/trauma

"I have swept away your offenses like a cloud,
    your sins like the morning mist.
Return to me,
    for I have redeemed you."

Sing for joy, you heavens, for the Lord has done this;
    shout aloud, you earth beneath.
Burst into song, you mountains,
    you forests and all your trees,
for the Lord has redeemed Jacob,
    he displays his glory in Israel.

Ultimately, Jesus fulfills this promise from God. He has made a way through his death on the cross for us to be restored to a fully Connected relationship with God (John 3:16-17). In his life on earth and in his death, he identified with our humanity and our struggles (Hebrews 4:15). His resurrection gives us hope of our own resurrection (1 Corinthians 15:20-22). And even more, Jesus promises us a life of freedom when we are Connected with him! (See John 10:1-11.)

What Is "Fitness?"

We love puzzles. Starting a new puzzle is a fun challenge, sorting pieces, looking for color themes, or edge frame pieces. But as it all slowly comes together, the beautiful image is revealed. The reward for hours, days, or even weeks of persistence is not just in the finished product but also the feeling of satisfaction in having completed it.

Unfortunately, our son's cat also loved puzzles, but the cat had a different idea of what to do with the pieces than we have, so we usually found ourselves frustrated a few days after starting a new puzzle! We would go to work on the puzzle and find pieces (or whole sections) knocked on the floor, potentially lost, or—most infuriating—chewed up. When a puzzle piece is chewed or broken, it doesn't fit, so the finished picture can never be complete.

Most of the time, you probably use the term "fit" to mean physically healthy. You probably think of fitness in terms of muscular strength, endurance, and possibly a specific weight or body fat percentage. However, it can also mean connected and connect-able, like a puzzle piece must be whole and the right shape to connect to the pieces around it. Without being able to connect appropriately, the piece doesn't "fit."

True "fitness" includes a healthy sense of Connection to God, your self, and the world around you, particularly your faith community. Healthy Connection to God involves giving and receiving, serving and being filled by Grace, loving and being loved. We were not meant to be like sponges that get wrung out and set aside only to become dried-up hard bricks. Rather, we were made to remain in relationship with God and others in a way that keeps us filled and overflowing. This is the meaning of the "living water" Jesus promises to give those who follow him (John 7:38).

Healthy Connection to your self also involves the principles we have already been discussing—awareness and Curiosity, leading to transformation. It never involves condemnation or disrespect of your self. You have been made in God's image! You, yourself, and everything about you were created to reflect who God is to the world. You reflect his image as an individual and also as part of the bigger picture God is creating. In that very truth, there is innate and inherent dignity. Believing, accepting, and living that truth is the essence of fitness. Even if you feel like the puzzle piece that has been chewed up and kicked under the sofa, God is always working to restore you to the beautiful creation he intends you to be.

A healthy Connection to your world involves living your purpose as God has created and gifted you. In this sense, fitness is about mutual care and service—giving of yourself while also receiving love and support from your sisters and brothers.

It is appropriate here to mention healthy boundaries. Finding your fit in community with others can be tricky when others want to treat you like a sponge and simply squeeze you out. When that is the case, it is appropriate to step back and ask whether you might need to establish boundaries to improve your Connection. Your puzzle piece has its own place. It's not okay for someone (even you) to try to shove you into the wrong place or to let yourself be turned around the wrong way. The more you learn who God has made you to be and how you fit into his picture, the easier it becomes to set these boundaries. Practice Curiosity as you seek healthy Connection so that you can land where God intends you to fit.

Ultimately when all of us, created in God's image, become appropriately Connected to God, ourselves, and others, we form the most beautiful of puzzles! God is working to fit us all together. He picks up the pieces that fall on the floor. He repairs and restores those that have been chewed on or broken. He diligently seeks out each and every lost or missing piece. In the end, God will reveal the most beautiful and glorious image of himself and his glory!

One day as we were talking with our friend Sarah, she shared how this had played out for her. She been battling fears and discouragement around some difficult relationships in her family. She struggled to believe that she was fully accepted and wanted to be able to communicate her love and support in a way that could be received by others. As she wrestled with her feelings in prayer, she became aware that she couldn't just sit and stew in them. She needed to release it all to God, but she still wasn't sure how. So she took one simple step and chose to go to the gym to work out. As she drove there, she received phone calls from her counselor and other family members to encourage her. The phone calls did more than just help her feel supported by people in her life. The timing of it all showed her that God saw her and cared about what she was experiencing in that very moment! While her relationship struggles didn't resolve right away, she found hope and was able to surrender her fears. God proved that he was bigger and able to meet her right in the middle of her pain. He has been slowly restoring her, showing her more clearly her fit not just in her family but also in the Body of Christ.

We encourage you to seek fitness in both senses. Seek to Thrive and become healthier in the areas we will discuss in the next section of this book. At the same time, seek to become Connected. God created and designed you very intentionally. There's an old saying that is worth repeating: God does not make any mistakes. With that in mind, pursue your own fit-ness, your sense of Connection.

Are you aware of whether you are experiencing Connection to God, others, and yourself? Americans tend to be highly isolated and individualistic, so it's possible that your sense of Connection and community may need further development. We often go through our days on autopilot, moving habitually from one thing to the next: get up, have a cup of coffee, get dressed, take the kids to school, go to work, do what's expected, come home, have dinner, watch TV, go to bed. This doesn't tend to lend to the kind of awareness that is necessary for healthy Connection. So here are some questions and suggestions to look at to help you grow in this area:

- At random moments in your day, stop and pay attention to what you are doing, what you are thinking, how you are interacting with others, and what you are feeling. You might even set alarms on your phone to go off every hour or so for a self-check.

- Ask who in your life really knows you. Who do you know well? Who can you disagree with in a way that honors both of you as individuals with unique perspectives?

- What does your relationship with God really look like? Do you ever experience God's love for you—and if so, what does his love feel like? When you do spend time with God, is it more personal or practical? Do you pray only asking for things, or can you also listen to his thoughts? Is your time in the Bible more focused on study and learning or on discovering and understanding who God is?

If you find you struggle with healthy Connection, we encourage you to remain hopeful. As you walk through the rest of this book, you'll be able to grow with small steps in various areas of your life. You can begin to make small, simple steps to grow in awareness. You may need to seek out a mentor or counselor to help you in this area. We'll offer more suggestions for you further on in this book. For now, be aware that Connection to God, yourself, and others is an important foundational principle in building Wellness in your life. This is an important tool to use in your growth, and if it's new to you, we will walk you through learning to use it.

CHAPTER 4

Grace: God's Power to Crush the Impossible

"What appears humanly impossible is more than possible with God."

Luke 18:27 TPT

"God's marvelous grace has manifested in person, bringing salvation for everyone. This same grace teaches us how to live each day... passionate to do what is beautiful in his eyes."

Titus 2:11-12a, 14b

In Portuguese, the beautiful word *saudade* doesn't really translate to English. Its literal meaning is "The feeling of longing for an absent something or someone that you love but might never return."[11] The

---

11: Martinique. "13 Beautiful Words with No English Translation ' Go Blog: EF United States." GO Blog | *EF United States*, EF Education First, www.ef.edu/blog/language/13-words-with-no-english-translation/. Accessed 9 Feb, 2023.

English word "grief" comes close, but it doesn't fully express the deep emotional longing for what has been loved and lost that is encompassed by saudade. This is often true in many languages—words that express a deep cultural concept just don't translate into other cultures and their languages.

In our studies, we've come to believe that the word "Grace" translates incompletely from the "culture" of who God is into any human language. In Greek, the word for "Grace" is *charis*, which means a gift or kindness, sometimes undeserved by the recipient. The Hebrew text of the Bible uses two words. *Hen* means grace, charm, favor, and popularity—being seen by others in a good light. *Hinnah* is generally used about God to mean "has shown favor, mercy, compassion or grace."[12] Simply using these definitions, Bible teachers generally conclude that "Grace" means God's gift to undeserving people of kindness, compassion, mercy, and favor. What an incredible gift! That we humans who have rejected God or tried to redefine God to fit our limited comprehension receive anything from the infinite Creator of the Universe is astounding.

But there's even more to Grace! A study not just of the word but of how it is used throughout the Scriptures shows that what Grace *does* is far greater than we've understood.

- Grace is God's favor to people, preferential treatment simply because God chooses to give it. Ezra 9:8-9 demonstrates this beautifully. God gave the Israelites favor from pagan Persian kings—kings who didn't even recognize YHWH as God—so that the people would

---

12: *Bible Word Study: Grace*, Logos: Deep Bible Study app version 28.0.4, Faithlife Corporation, Logos Bible Software, www.logos.com.

be able to return to their land, rebuild the temple, and rebuild the city of Jerusalem. God is especially inclined to show this kind of favor to those who are humble and oppressed (Proverbs 3:34, James 4:5-6).

- Grace preserves God's people. Again, the passage in Ezra 9 demonstrates how God "left a remnant" of the Israelites through the Babylonian conquest and exile. Romans 11:5-6 also refers to an ongoing, current "remnant chosen by grace," making it clear that this is by God's choice and not because of any human works.

- Grace gives people gifts (what we usually refer to as "spiritual gifts") to serve one another in the Body of Christ (Romans 12:6-8, 1 Peter 4:10-11).

- Grace empowers God's people, not only to serve one another through spiritual giftings, but in many other ways. Stephen and others were able to perform miraculous signs by God's Grace (Acts 6:8). Paul experienced this empowerment to work harder than other apostles (1 Corinthians 15:8-10) and to be strong in his weakness (2 Corinthians 12:9-10). God's people provide for the needs of others by Grace (Acts 4:33; 2 Corinthians 9:8, 14). Hebrews 4:15-16 reminds us to approach God's throne to receive Grace in our need.

- God's Grace provides salvation. By the power of Grace, we are rescued from a place of separation from and enmity towards God and brought into a relationship where we experience his love, kindness, compassion, and mercy. The New Testament is clear that we have no power on our own to please God by our human acts, and it is only through Grace that we can experience this eternal relationship with our Father in Heaven (Acts 15:10-11; Romans 3:23-24; Romans 5:15-21; Ephesians 1:5-6; Ephesians 2:6-10; Titus 2:11-12; Hebrews 2:9).

- But Grace doesn't stop its work with salvation! It transforms us more and more into who God intends for us to be. Grace changed Paul from a blasphemer into a faithful servant who spoke God's truth and convinced countless others of Jesus's deity (1 Timothy 1:12-14).

- By Grace, we each have a purpose and are likewise transformed from our old selves into "God's handiwork" so that we can fulfill that purpose (Ephesians 2:10).

- And as if all that weren't enough, God promises even more Grace to us at Jesus's return! (See 1 Peter 1:13.)

In all of this we see that Grace really is a far greater concept than most of us understand. Grace is God's power at work in the world. Grace is God's way of overcoming impossible obstacles and boundaries to accomplish his good purposes. It's both universal and personal. Through Grace, God is building, empowering, and transforming you while also using you and your experiences to accomplish something far bigger in the world and in all of human history. In all of this, God chooses undeserving people and bestows compassion, kindness, mercy, and favor to show his tremendous love and indescribable goodness.

Have you ever tried to make a change in your life but found yourself just going back to the way things were? No matter how badly you wanted or needed the change, something in you resisted the change, and you ended up back where you began. It's so frustrating!

Whether it's a mindset change, weight loss, ending a toxic relationship, beginning a new relationship, beginning (and sticking with) an exercise program, leaving a job, or any of a number of significant changes in life, the reality is that transformation is hard. According to Dr. Caroline Leaf, "most people hardly change in a five-year period and tend to get stuck for a long time!"[13] We need more than willpower to make and stick with significant changes in our lives.

Every coach and lifestyle guru has their own "mindset hacks" to help people overcome this stuck-ness and move forward in transformation. Genuine mental blocks keep us in uncomfortable "comfort" zones for years, even decades. It's crucial to uncover and release them, but how?

By God's Grace.

Grace gives you the strength to get up in the morning, to choose healthy foods, to forgive yourself when you don't meet your own expectations, to forgive others who hurt you, to set boundaries in relationships, to set aside time to pray and rest in God's presence, to change habits. By Grace, God enables and empowers you to do what he calls you to do.

Practically, though, how does that work? What does it look like? We'd like to offer a five-step model of transformation in life that relies on God's Grace. We believe that following these steps, using Curiosity and Connection, empowered by Grace, you can begin to experience breakthrough in areas where you may have been stuck for a long time. Keep this process in mind as you read through the next section of the book. God may point out something where you aren't living in

---

13: Dr. Leaf, Caroline. *Neurocycle*. Switch On Your Brain, LLC, v. 2.5.0, ©2022. www.neurocycle.app.

alignment with what he says is "Good." As you seek transformation in this area, instead of striving for change by "gutting it out," follow this process.

The Grace Cycle

This process, which we call The Grace Cycle, forms the foundation for experiencing transformation in our lives. Throughout the process, use Curiosity to be aware of how you are moving through it. You have the freedom to adapt or change what you're doing at any step. This is not a formula but a framework that you can use to fit your life. You will see throughout this process how Connection with God, others, and your own self remains essential. And remember to rely on God's Grace to empower you. Remember that Grace is how God works to overcome impossible obstacles to accomplish his purposes! Trust in his compassion and kindness while you rely on his power in your weakness.

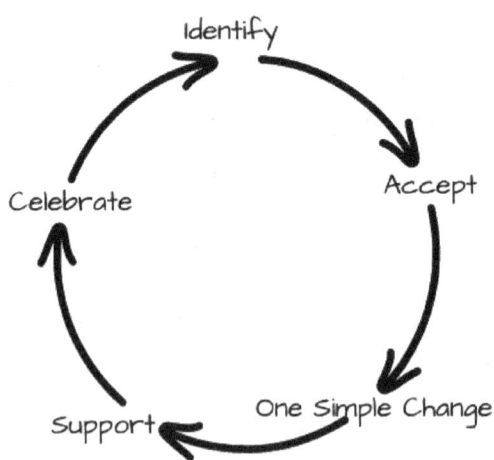

Step One: Identify an area for change

Take some time to pray and Connect with God and your self. This is crucial. Remember God's love and his Grace that gives you strength. From this place, aware that he sees you with love and not condemnation (Romans 8:1), ask God to reveal to you one area of your life that is not in line with what he wants for you—one area that isn't aligned to his calling towards Goodness. This doesn't need to be an area of sin or weakness. God may be calling you to a minor course correction to get back on the road he has for you. Remember that God loves you and wants the best for you... not *from* you but *for* you. God accepts you as you are now, and yet he also sees the amazing person you will become as you grow closer to him. Rest in that reality as you Identify an area for growth and change.

You may find something in the next section of this book that speaks strongly to you where you need to experience a change in your life. This may look like changing how you interact with your spouse or children, shifting your eating habits, dealing with a mental or emotional struggle, or a change to your work or spending habits. We encourage you to dig a little deeper into an issue that may be impacting other areas of your life. Don't rush this, but don't overthink it either. If you need to simply choose one thing to practice this process, then it's better to make a start than to wait until you've found the "perfect" thing to work on.

Step Two: Loving Acceptance

Most of us begin by gearing up for battle when we want to make a change in our lives. We enter into a mindset that wants to reject the past and move all out toward the future. This not only requires a lot of personal energy, but it also can increase feelings of stress as we enter into "fight mode."

Instead, we encourage you to enter gently into your transformation. For example, a few years ago, I found myself feeling ready to lose the extra weight I had gained through the stress of the COVID pandemic. But instead of starting where most people would by setting a goal, ridding the house of all "unhealthy" foods, and throwing myself into a highly disciplined diet, I first paused to accept how I had gotten to that point.

At the beginning of the lockdowns in 2020, our family was facing some highly stressful situations. Michael became sick and was unable to recover for six weeks. Our older daughter and her boyfriend reacted with such high anxiety to the state of the world that they were unable to care for her child and so began asking (and later simply expecting) daily childcare from us. Our kindergarten child had to be taught at home and hated the virtual interactions and lessons forced on her. Stressed out, I found myself frequently at the pantry indulging in "comforting" snacks, and the extra pounds began piling on. When I decided to work on losing that extra weight, I chose to talk to myself like I would talk to a close friend, acknowledging that life had been stressful, so my body had gone into a natural survival state and done what it was inclined to do for protection. I approached losing extra pounds from a place of gratitude rather than disgust.

Likewise, as you identify anything in your life that isn't in alignment with Goodness, take some time to identify the story behind how you got to that place. Become aware that the behaviors and attitudes you developed arose to protect you in some way. Remind yourself that they didn't come about through intentional self-sabotage but through finding ways to cope with suffering, stress, or wounds caused by others. Instead of rejecting a past that you cannot change, recognize that you had to learn to survive that past. Begin your transformation by loving yourself and entrusting your future to the God who sees you, loves you, and is ready to empower you.

Step Three: Choose One Simple Change

Have you ever recognized a need for change in an area of your life then jumped in to completely overhaul that area? You start to make many changes... but do you stick with them? It can be overwhelming! Instead of a complete overhaul, we encourage you to make small changes and make them one at a time.

In John 5, when Jesus showed up at the Pool of Bethesda, he found a man who had been trying for decades to change his life. He kept doing the one thing that he knew to do, and it never worked. Over and over, he kept trying to be the first in the pool to receive healing. Jesus didn't offer what the man thought he needed, though. The disabled man thought he needed someone to help him get in the pool before anyone else. Instead, Jesus gave him one simple instruction: get up and pick up your mat. As he obeyed, he found healing. Admittedly, it took a great deal of faith for the man to obey Jesus. While Jesus called him to one simple step, it wasn't necessarily an easy one.

Jesus only showed the man at the Pool of Bethesda the one next step to take. He didn't outline how the man was to live his life from then on. He didn't even tell the man to expect what was to come—the Pharisees were about to question him and persecute him because of his new healed life, and Jesus didn't tell him how to handle it. He just asked the man to obey one simple step. In the same way, God will probably only show you the one next step to take as you seek transformation in your life. Empowered by Grace, supported by Connection to God and others, and using your Curious awareness of your self, choose and act on one simple step. Trust that God will give you Grace and wisdom for whatever follows as you act on that simple step. It isn't always an easy step. But God promises his presence and Grace to fill and empower you to act, one step at a time.

Consider how choices you made in the past have shaped who you are and how you live today. Whether those choices have led you to positive or negative experiences, release any judgments you hold. This is a time to surrender to God and his love for you, remembering that he accepts you as you are right now. What *one* choice can you make today that will change your direction and lead you to a new destination in a month, a year, or five years?

You will act on this new choice empowered by God's Grace. Again, just as you don't need to overthink Identifying an area for change in your life, you don't need to overthink this choice. One step in a new direction will lead you on a different journey! And if you find you have chosen a step that isn't working out well for any reason, it's okay to come back to this and change your mind. Just don't give up!

Step Four: Find Support

Making One Simple Change in your life can feel like a lot. Don't do it alone! Remember the importance of Connection with your Community? It's time to call them in! Find one or a few people to support you in your transformation. Take the risk of sharing with someone the simple step you have chosen to take, and give them permission to ask you how things are going. Be careful to choose people who love and support you enough to be honest and not allow you to let yourself down. With this genuine support, you will be further empowered to continue your transformation.

We continue to come back to this concept of Connection to a supportive, loving Community because it is essential to change and growth in life. In *The Other Half of Church*, Jim Wilder (a Christian neuroscientist) and Michel Hendricks write, "Our brains draw life from our strongest relational attachments to grow our character and develop our identity... Our brains are designed to use our attachments to form our character."[14] Scientific evidence supports our claim that people are transformed in the context of loving Community through these relational attachments. One of the best ways to grow in an area where you struggle is to draw close to people who are already thriving in that area. Learn from them as you engage in life together. Let God show you through them how he can also change you.

If you need help choosing your One Simple Change, you can seek input from people you trust and who know you well. Ask honest questions as you seek out their wisdom. The quality of support you

---

14: "Hesed: Our Relational Glue." *The Other Half of Church*, Moody Publishers, Chicago, IL, 2020, Kindle Loc 1130.

receive will reflect the depth of your relationship with others. And if you don't have a truly supportive community, reach out to us at thriving@1fit.us.

Step Five: Celebrate your Wins!

Have you made progress? What specific changes have you seen in your life? Take a pause and celebrate! Thank God for what he is doing in your life. Share with your supportive Community! Go smile at yourself in the mirror and say, "Good job!" Write it down. Do this often! And don't wait until you see big changes in your life. Celebrate even the smallest shifts in your life.

Why? Is this really important? We believe this is a critical element of change for a number of reasons. First, it builds confidence and a growth mindset. Simply moving from one area where you feel "I need to change" to the next can cause you to believe messages such as "I'm not good enough." However, when you stop to celebrate your success, you embrace the messages of "I can do hard things" and "I am transforming and growing." Second, pausing to acknowledge and reflect on your wins can motivate you for the next stage. Finally, this will improve your healthy Connections to yourself, others, and even God. As you have relied on God's Grace throughout your work, return to him in gratitude to share your joy. You build Community with others by celebrating together. And you honor yourself and your hard work by celebrating yourself.

In our brains, the neurotransmitter dopamine helps us to feel pleasure and satisfaction. Celebration releases dopamine. When you experience this sense of satisfaction, it motivates you for the future—

this is how God created our brains. Don't short-circuit your progress by skipping this step. You are worth celebrating, and your people will be happy to celebrate with you! Rejoice to know that God is pleased with the new choices and habits in your life that help you grow closer to him.

Continually repeat the process. You began with Connection to your self and looked at your life with Curiosity to identify an area to work on. You lovingly accepted whatever happened in the past that led to the need for change. Empowered by God's Grace, you chose One Simple Change to work on. You found support from others as you worked on changing your behavior in this area. You paused to celebrate your successes. Now it's time again to look inside and ask what's next. Perhaps there's another step in this same area you feel led to take. Or maybe you recognize that another area of your life has been impacted by your history and needs some work. Remember that you get to decide what you're going to do for your self!

Maybe the next change will be easier because of the work you've already done. Or it might be more challenging because you've become more self-aware. God might lead you to tackle something deeper. Yet you've already grown in Wellness and learned new ways to experience his Grace. Remember what you have already accomplished and trust that God will be with you and continue to empower you!

Over time, you will notice that each simple change you incorporate into your life will add to what you've already done and will impact how you show up in greater ways. Growth becomes a lifelong process. You don't need to be anxious or try to rush this process. Let God show you what to work on in your life. At times you may need to just continue practicing and enjoying the Good things you have discovered in your life. You have the freedom to change directions at any time. But do so with an attitude of love towards yourself and in Grace. This will bring you freedom and joy as you grow in Wellness.

Part Two

The Seven Elements of Wellness

In this section of the book, we will look at seven areas of our lives and how to live in each area aligned with Wellness as the Bible describes it. We encourage you to seek to live in the most authentic and healthy way that you can: true to who God has made you to be, true to the principles laid out in the Bible (what we have been calling "Goodness"), and true to who you are as a unique individual. Live the way God has designed you to "fit" in the world. Remember that this is a process of growth. We don't intend for anything here to become a burden. Rather, we hope to encourage you to seek to align your life towards God's Good purpose for you, one simple step at a time.

In the coming chapters, we will describe what we mean by each of these areas and lay out a Bible-based vision for each one. We will offer some practical suggestions and questions to help you grow in that area. We will also (with one exception that you'll notice) invite you to consider how pain in your life in each area can point you towards what needs healing. Finally, to illustrate how to keep in mind Curiosity, Connection, and Grace, we'll present a case study for each area. These case studies are based loosely on real-life situations, and some are composites of a few people's stories. We hope to show you that you and God, working together, can make meaningful change in your life.

As you read, ask God to help you identify just *one* area for change in your life. Remain open and aware of what has and has not worked for you in the past. Seek out healthy community support and remember that God is with you. Tap into the power of God's Grace. Remember that your strength and ability to change come from him, not from your own power.

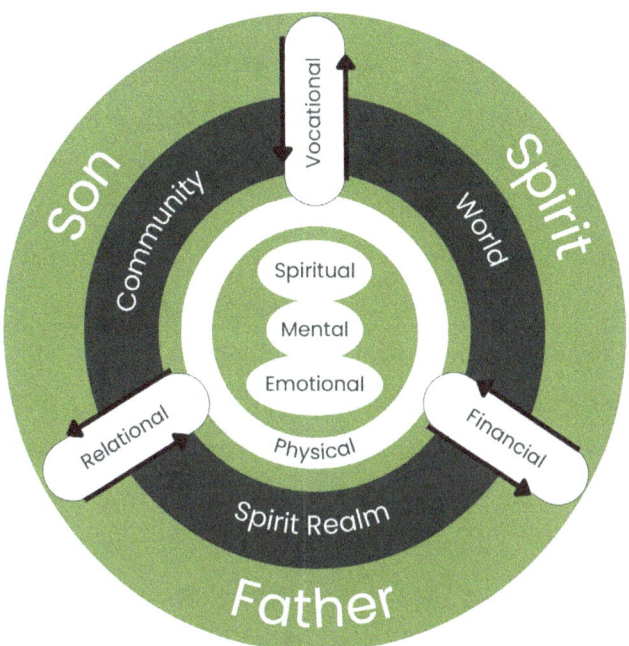

This diagram shows how we lay out these seven areas of life. Four are right at the center, the core of our selves. The Physical self encompasses the Spiritual, Mental, and Emotional Selves. These areas can be explored separately, but they also depend heavily on and influence one another. For our purposes here, we will look at them individually. However, be aware that changes in any of these areas will impact the others.

The other three elements—Relational, Vocational, and Financial—involve connections between our selves and what is outside of our selves. These are important for how you as a Physical/ Spiritual/Mental/Emotional person live in the world and live in God. You interact with your Community, the World, and the Spirit Realm through these areas of your life. It is also through these Connections that you interact with God in service and relationship. At the same time, God works through these three Connecting parts of our lives to help us identify areas of need and to bring Grace to our Core Selves. This is why the ovals for these three areas extend from the Core Self through the outside world to God with arrows pointing both outward and inward. For the moment, be aware of how this dynamic works. As you move forward, you'll understand it better.

You might ask why we chose these three specific areas of Connection to explore in this book. To begin with, these are all addressed extensively in the Bible. If you look at Jesus's Sermon on the Mount in Matthew 5-7, his practical teachings are about Relationships as well as our Mental and Emotional states. God also cares deeply about our Vocations—not only our work for pay but also our service to others. You'll see how much the Bible teaches about this area. Finances are so deeply intertwined into all parts of our lives that Michael uncovered most of the scriptures about this area as he studied the other areas! Not only are these three all areas that God's Word speaks to at length, but they are areas where we sense very deeply whether we are Thriving or simply surviving. No one can live in isolation from others, without any work/service, or free of financial needs or obligations. This is why we chose these specific areas to focus on.

You might think of other related areas of life to explore, such as prayer or sexuality. These are valid expressions of our selves as humans and as children of God. These are also areas where the Core Self and a Connecting part overlap. Prayer, for example, is an expression of the inner Spiritual self through Relationship with God and the Spirit Realm. Similarly, sexuality encompasses the Physical self along with varying degrees of the Core self expressed in the context of Relationship. Overall, we believe that if you look at the principles we will lay out in this section, you'll find that they show up in all other areas of life.

We are fully aware that each of these areas of life deserves a book of its own—and many books have been written to cover them! Our intent here is to look at a general overview and suggest some overarching Biblical principles related to each one. Most of the principles we lay out here have been formed from integrating teachings throughout the Bible. Where possible, we will cite specific verses and passages to support them. Throughout this section, we will help you to use Curiosity, Connection, and Grace to begin to experience transformation in your own life in these areas. With all of that in mind, let's dive into each one.

CHAPTER 5

The Core Four: Who I Am

"Love the Lord your God with all your heart and
with all your soul and with all your mind and
with all your strength."

Mark 12:30

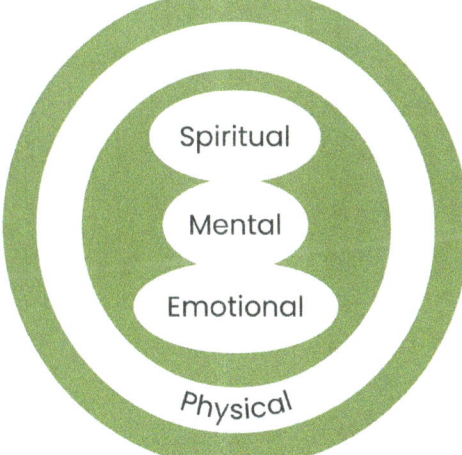

Physical Wellness

One evening at bedtime, I said something to one of my kids about her body, and she responded, "What is my body?" Children ask the most simple yet insightful questions at times, don't they? She was basically asking me to define her physical self, so I told her, "It's this part of you on the outside that holds all of what *you* are." That's the simple truth: your body is the physical container for all of what you are. For many in the "Health, Wellness and Fitness" industry, this is all they focus on, but we want to look at it in context of our whole selves. We acknowledge that we are drawing some lines here that in reality aren't all that firm. For example, our brains are part of our physical bodies, but they are also the seat of our mental and emotional selves. Still, with that in mind, we can look at some important guiding principles for Wellness in this area.

Let's look at the Biblical background and teachings about our physical self. Going all the way back to the beginning, Genesis 2:7 says "Then the LORD God formed man of dust from the ground, and breathed into his nostrils the breath of life; and man became a living being."[15] Psalm 139 reminds us that God forms our bodies from conception in our mothers' wombs. Our physical bodies are made by God and given to us by him. It's almost ridiculous to imagine a living person without a physical body, isn't it? But we need to begin by acknowledging this foundational truth. God made our physical selves, our bodies. We cannot have made them ourselves. They are neither accidents nor the result of random circumstances. As a gift from him,

---

15: Furthermore, Genesis 1:27 points out that God created male and female both in his image, equally valuable in his eyes.

our bodies are to be stewarded just as all gifts and resources from him.

In the New Testament, there are two primary words used to describe the physical self: *soma* and *sarx*. *Soma* describes the physical, mortal body; the seat of our senses, experiences, and suffering; the "part" of us that functions in human activity. *Sarx* describes the natural flesh as opposed to the spiritual; our body of brokenness and propensity to sin; the physically limited substance of humanity. *Sarx* is most often translated "flesh," while *soma* is generally translated "body." Paul uses both words when he talks about the resurrection of our physical bodies in 1 Corinthians 15:35-40, 44:

> But someone will ask, "How are the dead raised? With what kind of body [*soma*] will they come?" How foolish! What you sow does not come to life unless it dies. When you sow, you do not plant the body [*soma*] that will be, but just a seed, perhaps of wheat or of something else. But God gives it a body [*soma*] as he has determined, and to each kind of seed he gives its own body [*soma*]. Not all flesh [*sarx*] is the same: People have one kind of flesh [*sarx*], animals have another, birds another and fish another. There are also heavenly bodies [*soma*], and there are earthly bodies [*soma*]; but the splendor of the heavenly bodies [*soma*] is one kind, and the splendor of the earthly bodies [*soma*] is another... it is sown a natural body; it is raised a spiritual body.

A few fascinating points can be drawn from this passage. First, that humans are made of a different substance than animals, birds or fish. The nature of our *sarx* defines the experience of our life and sets humanity apart from other creatures that God has made. Second, that we have a physical body now *and* we will have a different kind of physical body after we die and are raised in resurrection. Finally, we might conclude that the future spiritual (yet somehow still physical) body will no longer be limited by the *sarx* that draws us into sin.

Furthermore, our physical bodies carry within them the limitations of broken humanity that have been inherited from Adam and Eve due to sin. These limitations are not only physical; they are also spiritual as they are drawn to sin and self-destruction. Paul describes this struggle in Romans 6-8, a battle that is a normal experience for those of us who seek to follow God's direction: we *know* what is right and how to live, but our *flesh*, part of our physical bodies, is continually drawn away from doing what is right. This is the nature of temptation! A key element of living in Biblical Wellness is learning to discern which desires come from God and which come from our flesh. (Learning that discernment happens as you walk with the Holy Spirit and seek growth in this area.)

Yet, beautifully, Jesus also took on flesh (*sarx*) and became human as we are. Hebrews 4:15 reminds us that Jesus understands our weakness because he was tempted in every way just as we are; however, because he did not succumb to sin, he can stand as a perfect High Priest and intercessor for us. He can also give us the grace we need in our times of temptation and need.

So with all of this background, what does Physical Wellness look like?

A familiar passage can guide us: "Do you not know that your bodies are temples of the Holy Spirit, who is in you, whom you have received from God? You are not your own; you were bought at a price. Therefore honor God with your bodies" (1 Corinthians 6:19-20). Physical Wellness at its root is honoring God with your body.

It is helpful to look at the full context here as well. In verses 12-15a, Paul says:

> "I have the right to do anything," you say—but not everything is beneficial. "I have the right to do anything"—but I will not be mastered by anything. You say, "Food for the stomach and the stomach for food, and God will destroy them both." The body, however, is not meant for sexual immorality but for the Lord, and the Lord for the body. By his power God raised the Lord from the dead, and he will raise us also. Do you not know that your bodies are members of Christ himself?

He then goes on to strongly discourage sexual sin, concluding with, "All other sins a person commits are outside the body, but whoever sins sexually sins against their own body" (v. 18). I think we can safely expand this truth to other sins against our own bodies, such as drug and alcohol abuse and other forms of self-harm. Today, it's common to say, "But I'm not hurting anyone but myself!" to excuse such sins, but Paul's teaching clearly shows that we are harming not only ourselves but the presence of the Holy Spirit within us through self-harm. It's just not okay.[16]

16: Furthermore, in attachment relationships with others, anything I do that harms me also harms others.

What might it look like to honor God by treating our bodies as temples for his very presence? How does this responsibility, to be a physical home for the Holy Spirit, feel to you? Is it beautiful and honoring, or is it weighty, a heavy responsibility? Take some time to reflect on this reality and how it impacts you. We don't want you to move on too quickly from this awareness.

Now that you're aware of the value of your physical body as God's home, his temple, let's explore three primary principles around Physical Wellness.

Principles of Physical Wellness

Physical Wellness is stewardship of the body God has given you.

Your body serves three important purposes. First, it is the home for your inner self. It serves as the container for your mind, heart, and soul. As such, it is the place where you connect with the Holy Spirit. If you have a relationship with God, his Spirit lives within your physical body. Unlike the times when God revealed his presence in a Tabernacle or Temple, you don't need to go anywhere to experience God's presence. He is present within you at all times and in all places! Simply opening your heart and mind to his presence is all that is necessary to connect with God.

Furthermore, your body is a tool or a vehicle to serve and honor God. Paul instructed in Romans 6:13, "offer every part of yourself to him as an instrument of righteousness." Consider your body as an instrument or tool. How will you choose to use it? To honor and serve God and others with your body is Physical Wellness. (You can serve God in many ways, which you can explore when we look at

Vocational Wellness. For now, just be aware of the simple yet obvious truth that you serve God using your body.)

Physical Wellness relies on the Spirit of God to overcome the desires and weakness of our corrupted flesh to build strength so that we can do the good things He has made us for.

Remember that physically we are both *soma* and *sarx*, meaning we have limitations and also a propensity to follow temptation into sin and self-destruction. If that were the only truth about our physical selves, we would (understandably) fall into utter hopelessness. But God gives us strength in our weakness! Remember that Jesus suffered temptation just as we do. He calls us to approach him for Grace to overcome in our time of need (Hebrews 4:15-16). Consider Paul's weakness that he describes in 2 Corinthians 12. He had a physical limitation of some kind that caused him torment. He pleaded with God three times to remove it from him—imagine the frustration of this man who God used to heal others regularly being unable to experience healing himself! Yet when he talked to God about this torment and God's inexplicable refusal to heal him, God answered, "My grace is sufficient for you, for my power is made perfect in weakness" (2 Corinthians 12:9). Experiencing God's Grace and empowerment in and through his physical limitations allowed Paul to reframe his experience and be able to say, "For when I am weak, then I am strong" (2 Corinthians 12:10). Isn't it beautiful that Paul said, "When I am weak, then *I* am strong"—not "*he (God)* is strong."

By God's Grace, you can experience strength in the midst of weakness. Reliance on God's Spirit allows you to overcome the

71

limitations of *sarx* that so easily drops into sin and dishonoring the Holy Spirit within you. It also strengthens you to serve him according to his design even when you are limited. Whether your limitations stem from a health struggle or a battle against the flesh, his Grace given to you through the Holy Spirit can give you strength. In that, you and others see him at work powerfully!

Physical Wellness today is a taste of the glory to be experienced when God exchanges our bodies made of earth for bodies made of heaven.

As mentioned before, you were created to live on earth in a physically limited body, yet your inner self will also have a future eternal existence in a non-limited, glorious, spiritual body (1 Corinthians 15:44). Have you ever experienced an adrenaline rush as the result of intense physical exercise? This may be a small taste of the glorious experience of a fully capable and energized heavenly body. Most of us know that the more we care for our physical bodies, the less we may be limited physically. Even though aging can begin to sap our physical abilities, we can continue to experience health and vitality. (As a fitness instructor who works largely with adults over 65 years old, I have seen this often.)

And yet you may be living with a chronic condition that causes you pain or weakness. We honor that your body may not give you any taste of the glory that awaits you at this point in your life. If you have "good days," we encourage you to not simply accept those as a day of relief from your ongoing struggles. You can also let those days remind you of the complete healing that God holds for you when you meet him face to face. We understand this because we both live with bouts of physical pain, making us often aware of environmental and diet triggers that can cause the pain to erupt. We encourage you to continue pursuing growth in Physical Wellness through awareness of things that make you feel better or worse.

Using Physical Pain to Identify Areas of Need

For the most part, we humans are good at naming our physical pains. How often have you heard (or said), "Oh, my head hurts!" or "Ugh, my stomach" or something similar? You know where you hurt. Even if your immediate response is to reach for the Ibuprofen or antacids, you do so because you recognize pain. Author Phillip Yancey deals with this subject in a number of his books such as *Pain: The Gift that Nobody Wants* and *When Life Hurts: Understanding God's Place in Your Pain*. The titles of these books speak volumes. Pain—or at least the ability to feel pain—is a gift from God. Yancey and Dr. Paul Brand have written often of Hansen's Disease (more commonly known as leprosy). Dr. Brand discovered that leprosy is not a skin disease but a nerve disease that destroys a person's ability to feel pain.[17] A person who cannot feel pain must be constantly vigilant because even a small injury like a splinter can lead to a life-threatening infection when left untreated. Pain calls attention to your needs, sometimes rather insistently. Pain is not God's punishment but instead a way of calling you to awareness of something wrong so that you can address it. In Michael's case, for example, the persistent and intense pain of arthritis with no known cause or effective treatment eventually led to

---

17: Yancey, Philip. "The Holy Disease." *Philip Yancey*, 8 Dec. 2019, philipyancey.com/the-holy-disease.

a diagnosis of Celiac Disease and an understanding that inflammation caused by gluten had been causing his pain.

Likewise, your physical pain symptoms may be pointing to a deeper issue in your body. Please do not take any of our advice over that of a physician who has been treating you. However, we encourage you to explore whether your diet, some environmental sensitivity, or even muscle tightness could be a factor in any pain you're experiencing. Pay careful attention to anything that increases your pain or relieves it. Remember that you are the expert on you. We are not encouraging you to avoid treating any painful symptoms you experience, but to become Curious and aware of them. Don't let the pain lead you away from Connection to God or your self. Instead, lean in, trusting in God's presence to guide you and his Grace to help you move towards health and Wellness.

Practical Suggestions

To put all of this into practice, begin by laying aside habits that don't reflect good stewardship of your body. If you discover that you aren't honoring God with your body in some way, let us offer some very practical applications of how to grow in Physical Wellness. It is important to build physical health and strength today. When you begin to Thrive in this area, you are better able to honor and serve God with your body. Furthermore, you may experience tastes of the future God has for you in a glorified body through good health in your earthly body.

We will suggest some specific areas where you might be able to improve your Physical Wellness. Remember to use Curiosity to explore what is right for *you* as a unique individual. Remain Connected to yourself in awareness, to God for guidance, and to others for support and accountability. Allow God's Grace to empower you as you begin to make One Simple Change (if this is an area where God is leading you to seek transformation). We'll take a fairly high-level view of all of these, just enough to help you uncover something that may need to shift in how you care for your body. At the end of the chapter, you can take some time to reflect on all of this using the questions we provide. The four areas we'll look at are nutrition, movement, rest, and professional support.

Nutrition

Keeping in mind that every person has different nutrition needs, cultural preferences, and food sensitivities, we aren't about to prescribe any specific diet plan. Even the US Dietary Guidelines published by the USDA and HHS specifically say, "The Guidelines also explicitly emphasize that a healthy dietary pattern is not a rigid prescription. Rather, the Guidelines are a customizable framework of core elements within which individuals make tailored and affordable choices that meet their personal, cultural, and traditional preferences."[18] In general, healthy nutrition focuses heavily on whole fruits and vegetables for nutrients and fiber along with healthy protein sources. Avoid added sugars and solid fats. There's no one perfect "diet" or eating lifestyle

---

18: Dietary Guidelines for Americans 2020-2025, US Department of Health and Human Services with Office of Disease Prevention and Health Promotion, p. viii, http://dietaryguidelines.gov., accessed 4/6/2023.

other than being certain to take in foods that help your body feel its best.

Use your Curiosity to pay attention to how foods that you eat make you feel. If you suspect a specific food is causing digestive problems or extreme fatigue, try eliminating it for about two weeks and then reintroduce a small amount to see if it's a culprit. It's also possible that multiple foods may be causing troubles. If that's the case, you might work with a professional such as a registered dietitian, a nutritionist, or a functional medicine practitioner to help you.

Movement

Physical Activity is essential to maintaining health, yet again there is no single prescription for exercise that is best for everyone. In general, experts recommend about 150 minutes each week of moderately intense activity (anything that elevates your heart rate) plus two weekly sessions of muscle-strengthening exercise.[19] Yet other research has shown that any physical activity, even standing up and walking around the house or office, has a positive effect on health.[20] Engaging as often as you can in some kind of movement that you enjoy is essential. Ask yourself what you enjoy, try new things, and discover what works for you.

19: "How Much Physical Activity Do Adults Need?" US Centers for Disease Control, https://www.cdc.gov/physicalactivity/basics/adults/index.htm, accessed 4/6/2023.
20: "Studies Find Even Minimal Physical Activity Measurably Boosts Health," UC San Diego Health, https://health.ucsd.edu/news/press-releases/2020-10-12-studies-find-even-minimal-physical-activity-measurably-boosts-health/, accessed 4/6/2023.

However, you need to move your body! One of my class members, Amelia, tells the story of how she fell on a slippery sidewalk, causing bilateral sciatic pain. She spent a few days in bed trying to rest up, but over time, the pain increased to the point where she could barely move, even with a walker. After a few months, she reached the point of asking her sons to put her in a nursing home, but they refused! Instead, they encouraged her to do what the doctors had recommended: moving her body. Despite excruciating pain, she began doing just a few simple exercises once a day. After a few weeks, she was able to do more, then go to physical therapy and eventually give up the walker. Now, even with daily pain in both legs, Amelia participates in exercise classes five days a week and has a full life, determined not to let the pain slow her down.

Rest

When talking about rest, we include sleep as well as finding ways to incorporate rest into your day. Sleep itself is a dynamic state during which our bodies grow and restore tissue while our minds process thoughts that generally lie below our conscious awareness. Adults need seven to nine hours of sleep each night, yet at least 30 percent of Americans don't sleep enough.[21] If you are able to sleep enough to help you feel rested and energized throughout your day, you're doing well! If not, here are some suggestions.

21: The State of Sleep Health in America 2023, American Sleep Apnea Association, https://www.sleephealth.org/sleep-health/the-state-of-sleephealth-in-america/, accessed 6/1/2023.

Sleep experts talk about the importance of certain habits in getting the most restful sleep. These include the following:

- keep your bedroom quiet, dark, and at a comfortable temperature
- avoid screens before bed
- maintain a regular sleep schedule
- avoid alcohol before sleep (yes, it can make you feel tired, but it actually interferes with restful sleep throughout the night)
- expose yourself to sunlight in the morning to help reset circadian rhythms

If you're not getting enough restful sleep at night, consider whether you might be able to make one or two changes from the list above. If these do not improve your sleep, then you might need to seek a doctor or sleep therapist for additional help. You might also need to look at whether a nutrient deficiency or hormonal imbalance is causing your sleep problems. Stay Curious and persist in finding the answer for you.

In addition to adequate sleep at night, your mind and body need times of restoration during the day. This might look like a 20-minute "power nap." Or maybe you can take five to seven minutes for meditation during your day. Meditation can take many different forms. Some people benefit greatly from taking some time to just let their minds wander while others benefit from periods of complete mental and physical stillness and silence. Even if your lifestyle leads you to feel like you need to go nonstop through your day without any breaks, we encourage you to find a few minutes here and there to stop and take a few breaths. Rest is essential to your physical health!

Professional Support

Sometimes we experience physical issues that we simply cannot solve on our own, no matter how connected and curious we are with our own bodies. At times we must seek the help of a professional to support our optimal physical health. There is no shame in seeking outside help, whether it be from a doctor, a registered dietitian, a personal trainer, a naturopathic doctor, or any other professional in this area. Above all, partner with professionals who recognize that you know your own body better than anyone else. If anyone dismisses your experience and your awareness of how your body is responding to a prescribed treatment, give yourself permission to move on and find someone else. You are the only one who will live in your body! Choose to be loyal to your self before you are loyal to any professional you have partnered with.

Questions to Ask in Pursuit of Physical Wellness

- How well am I honoring God with my Physical body?
- What are the temptations that my flesh (*sarx*) leans towards most often? What can I change to avoid succumbing to these temptations?
- How do the foods I usually eat make me feel? Could there be a food I eat that makes me feel worse or better?

(Possibly use a food log or journal to help you make a connection between food and energy.)

- What movement makes me feel good and energized? What time of day feels best for me to exercise? If I'm not happy with my physical activity, what can I try to do differently?

- Do I wake up feeling rested most days? If not, what can I change to help me sleep better? Do I need to incorporate rest in my day to help me keep going?

As you consider these questions, you might identify One Simple Change you can make to begin to experience greater Physical Wellness. Share that choice with someone who will support and encourage you. Continue to seek Grace to empower you and transform you.

Physical Wellness Case Study

Bess battled losing the same 20 pounds over and over for years. After her third pregnancy at 42 years old, she found it harder to return to her pre-pregnancy weight. She had counted calories, started walking every day, and cut out all carbs from her eating. This helped her until her mom was diagnosed with cancer and Bess found herself eating for comfort and stress relief. After her mom's cancer went into remission, Bess returned to her previous diet only to find the extra weight harder to lose this time. When her friend lost 45 pounds on a popular weight-loss system, Bess signed up. Shakes, snacks, meals… everything she put in her mouth was carefully prescribed, prepared, and portioned, and she did drop the 20 pounds over the course of a few months. But within a year after she stopped using the system, she had regained the weight. Frustrated, she began to wonder whether she was dealing with perimenopause and would just have to live with being overweight for the rest of her life.

One spring, Bess joined a missions trip to India. As an act of love and sensitivity to those they served, her team adopted a largely vegetarian diet for the two weeks of their service. Bess noticed after just a couple of days that she had more energy than normal and didn't feel the need for her afternoon coffee like she usually did at home. She had heard people talk about the benefits of vegan and vegetarian diets, but she generally wrote it off as unrealistic because she believed she needed more protein in her diet than she could get without consuming meat. She noticed her pants feeling looser in the last few days she spent in India, but she attributed any weight loss to eating fewer calories.

Still, she couldn't argue with what happened the first time she had a salad with a grilled chicken breast at home. She felt bloated all evening, then started the next day feeling almost too tired to get out of bed. So she decided to try eliminating meat from her diet for another few days while still eating a normal caloric intake to see if that would make a difference. Her energy levels jumped back up within days! This led her to do more research about vegetarianism, and she reached out to a friend who she knew didn't eat meat. She realized it would be difficult to eliminate meat when she was preparing meals for her husband and children. But with prayer and the new understanding she had gained, she began to make small adaptations to her own meals. She ate meat on occasion and found new ways to bring fish into her family's meals. A new variety of vegetables began showing up on their plates, and everyone found some that they enjoyed despite their expectations. Bess enjoyed eating food as she exercised her creativity and didn't limit herself to salads, chicken, and a few other things. Her weight dropped—not the full 20 pounds she wanted to lose, but enough to help her feel healthy. And she found new energy to serve her family at home as well as her faith community, serving as an assistant to the church's mission pastor to plan other mission trips and train volunteers.

Bess's story shows the Aha Moment that led her to Curiosity about her eating habits. She had tried to follow prescribed plans and things that worked for other people, but she didn't find success that way. Her realization came unexpectedly, but it happened through awareness of how she felt both by eating a meat-free diet and by eating meat again. She used Connection when she reached out to a friend to help her navigate this change, and she made sure to involve her family rather than making her own meals different from everyone else's. She used One Simple Change—reducing how much meat she ate—rather than a major overhaul. God's Grace subtly but powerfully infuses this entire story. In the context of serving through a missions trip, God brought to her awareness this simple dietary change. Ultimately, Bess grew in health and energy, enabling her to serve God and others. She found a new sense of joy and acceptance in her physical body.

Please note the point of this story is not to promote a vegetarian or vegan diet. To do so would be prescribing one choice as the one that should work for everyone. We simply use this to illustrate the power of Curiosity and One Simple Change to build Physical Wellness.

Spiritual Wellness

You might ask why we opened with addressing Physical Wellness when arguably Spiritual Wellness is more important and in a sense foundational to overall well-being. We began by looking at the Physical because it's the container for our core selves. Without a physical container, there is no place for the rest. Sometimes our physical selves are not healthy for many reasons that are beyond our conscious choices. When this happens (due to chronic disease, pain, injury, or other causes), the rest *may* suffer—but it doesn't have to. You are faced with a critical choice: will you turn towards God in trust or away from God by blaming him? Only one of those choices leads to true Connection with God and your self. While we always encourage you to trust God on the path to healing, we also know that Jesus warned us that while on this earth we will have trouble (John 16:33a). God may or may not have healing for you, but he does ask you to trust in him. Jesus said, "Take heart! I have overcome the world" (John 16:33b). In the midst of your troubles, whether your pain and suffering is physical or lies in another area, Jesus offers you peace.

Let's define the Spiritual Self before going any further. It is the immaterial (nonphysical) part of our selves that enables us to be connected to God and others. We base this definition on two things. First, the words used in both the Old Testament (*ruach*) and the New Testament (*pneuma*) mean spirit, breath, or wind. These are nonphysical. As for the connection part, in Genesis 2:7 we see that our very life-breath has been given to us by God. Through our Spirits, our very life, we experience connection to God and are able to connect with others.

While some might make the distinction that the Spiritual self alone is eternal, we disagree. We have already seen that God promises us a future Physical existence, although in a different "heavenly" type of body. We believe that we all will still have mental and relational capabilities in that eternal body.[22] In a redeemed relationship with God, we can experience growing Wellness in this area. As we strengthen our Spiritual selves, we begin to Thrive in all areas, just as strengthening our physical muscles helps to improve other areas of our physical health.[23]

Spiritual Wellness is reflecting the image of God more fully in your spirit, just as growing in every area of your life causes you to live a life more like Jesus's life. In your spirit, this looks like the fruit of the (Holy) Spirit that Paul describes in Galatians 5:22-23: love, joy, peace, patience, kindness, goodness, faithfulness, gentleness, and self-control. In Galatians 5, Paul contrasts this with behaviors that are led by the passions and desires of the flesh. He points out that we can bear this good fruit in our lives by walking in step with the Holy Spirit (v. 16, 25).

What does it look like to walk in step with the Holy Spirit? Jesus said in John 15:1-5:

> I am the true sprouting vine, and the farmer who
> tends the vine is my Father. He cares for the branches

22: To illustrate this, you can look at the torment of hell, experiencing disconnection from God (and presumably from others) while also experiencing physical pain (see Luke 16:19-31).

23: However, while physical strength doesn't last, spiritual strength that we develop in life does remain!

connected to me by lifting and propping up the fruitless branches and pruning every fruitful branch to yield a greater harvest. The words I have spoken over you have already cleansed you. So you must remain in life-union with me, for I remain in life-union with you. For as a branch severed from the vine will not bear fruit, so your life will be fruitless unless you live your life intimately joined to mine. I am the sprouting vine, and you're my branches. As you live in union with me as your source, fruitfulness will stream from within you—but when you live separated from me, you are powerless. (TPT)

Jesus made a very clear promise here: as you "live in union" with him (a phrase translated as "abide" in the NIV and elsewhere), you will bear fruit in your life (v. 5). The only requirement is to be Connected in relationship with Jesus.

Jesus talks about two kinds of branches in this passage, and it's important to note that both of these types *are connected to him*. These branches represent people who have a relationship with Jesus. First, he addresses those who are not currently bearing fruit. Most modern English translations have made an unfortunate word choice here, usually saying he "takes away" or "cuts off" these branches, which is why we especially like how The Passion Translation says that the Father lifts and props up branches that aren't fruitful.[24] Grape

---

24: The Greek word used here, airo, means "take away; take up; pick up" (*Bible Word Study*: lifting, Logos: Deep Bible Study app version 28.0.4, Faithlife Corporation, Logos Bible Software, www.logos.com). It is also used in Acts 4:24, "they lifted their voices to God" and Revelation 10:5, "the angel... lifted up his right hand to heaven." The translations that say "cutting off" branches are not supported by this word.

vines need to be lifted up and tied to a strong support where they can receive sunlight in order to produce their fruit. In the same way, God picks up those whose lives aren't fruitful and places them where they can begin to Thrive. He doesn't leave his beloved ones lying in the dirt, nor does he throw them away. If your life is not currently showing the fruit of the Spirit—and this may be because of immaturity or due to choices that have drawn you away from God—ask God to lift you up and provide the support you need so you can bear fruit in your life.

Other branches are already fruitful, and the Father treats these differently. He prunes them so that they will yield even more fruit. He removes parts that are draining away the strength of the branch. But notice that the fruitful branch cannot prune itself any more than the fruitless branch can lift itself up. The fruit grows simply because it is connected to the life-giving source, the vine, not because of the branch's efforts. Spiritual Wellness is living a life like Jesus's by living Connected to him and seeing him produce fruit in your life.

Principles of Spiritual Wellness

God is Wholly Good, Loving, Wise, and Powerful.

Jesus illustrated this in John 10. He gave his life to bring us into the flock. He is the Good Shepherd; unlike a hired hand who would abandon the sheep to save himself, Jesus stands to protect and defend his flock.

However, your circumstances may lead you to question God's goodness and love. How can we reconcile this truth with the depth of human suffering in this world: wars, children who die of cancer, terrorism, addiction, even random accidents that cause painful lifelong disability? God doesn't give us answers to these questions, but as we said earlier, your choice is whether you will trust him, even in suffering and grief. How you respond to suffering and grief can reveal your level of Spiritual Wellness. We offer no judgment in this, only an opportunity to examine your own heart.

Ultimately in order to Thrive in this area of your life, you need to accept and trust this principle. God is good. He loves you (see Psalm 103). He does have a wise plan for not only your life but for the whole world. He is working all things for good, both for his glory and to shape you into the glorious person he created you to be (Romans 8). By his Grace, he will accomplish this, and he calls you to trust Him.

Through trust in Jesus Christ, we are awakened to experience Connection with God.

Jesus said, "I came that they [his sheep] may have life, and have it to the full" (John 10:10). He made it clear that his sheep are those who know his voice and follow him because they entered into his flock through him, the gate (John 10:9). Jesus is the Good Shepherd who laid down his life for his sheep through his death and resurrection. By his choice and his authority and in line with his Father's plan, he laid down his life and took it up again (John 10:18). In doing so, he made a way for you to become part of his flock. Taking this first step of trust in Jesus as the one who opens the gate for you creates the Connection with him that produces an abundance of fruit.

*Abundant life, freedom, and transformation occurs only
in continued Connection with God by faith.*

The Fruit of the Spirit as described in Galatians 5 is only part of the fruit of a life Connected to God through Jesus. As a whole, this fruit looks like abundance, transformation, and freedom. You can experience the abundance of blessings on earth as well as the eternal blessings of heaven (Ephesians 1:18-19, Ephesians 2:4-7). You are being continually renewed and transformed into the Image of Christ. (See Romans 8, Colossians 3, and 1 Peter 1.) And you can walk in freedom from sin (Romans 6).

We think of this as mutual delight and service with God. In any relationship, growth and connection are deeper when both people enjoy and support one another. This is the same in our relationship with God. It's not a simple back-and-forth where we accept God's love and respond with thanksgiving and service. Your life will be changed when you open yourself up to experiencing God's love and delight in you just as you are right now. His love extends far beyond the limited concept most of us hold as "the God who loved me enough to send Jesus to die for me." Transformation happens when you begin to see God as the one who is always present and longing for you to see him, always available with kindness and Grace, always rooting for you to succeed. He doesn't simply watch and control your life circumstances from afar. He walks with you, looking at you with delight! When you turn to him and see his face, you might be surprised at how big his smile is!

Mutual delight happens when two people simply enjoy each other's company. Mutual service comes from awareness of one another's needs and a desire to meet those needs because you want the best for one another. Do you know that God wants to serve you just as you serve him? He is a tenderhearted father who longs to scoop you up and comfort you when you fall. He offers support when you seek to serve others on his behalf. He doesn't ask you to do it all on your own. He serves and equips you as you serve him—you are not left to figure out how to serve on your own. If you have been feeling burned out on service, we encourage you to ask God where he is as you serve. You might be surprised to find that he was right next to you for a long time, offering a hand of support and love that you never recognized.[25]

Moving into life with God, experiencing mutual delight with God, brings freedom and abundant life. This is the life you long for, a life that is not characterized by a sense of striving that can lead to burnout or questioning your purpose. If you don't feel you're experiencing this mutual delight with God, then seek out his presence. Find a quiet space to sit and ask him where he is with you. If you've never done this before, it might feel strange or awkward. Trust him to show you, to show up for you. He has desired for a long time for you to ask.

Using Spiritual Pain to Identify Areas of Need

Unfortunately, we cannot identify Spiritual pain as easily as we do Physical pain. (Have you ever said, "Oh, my aching soul!"?) But maybe you have experienced the deep pain of isolation inside the shell of your soul—feeling that your prayers bounce off the ceiling, doubting whether God cares or even sees your hurts. You see unbearable

---

25: Further on when we discuss Vocational Wellness, we'll help you explore whether you may need to serve in a different way that is more appropriate.

suffering in the world and question God's goodness. Maybe you're barely hanging on to your faith but dare not utter the words in your mind, "I honestly don't know any more if God is even real." This kind of Spiritual pain can also look like bitterness over a hurt that won't go away. You might experience self-loathing over sinful thoughts or actions that you can't control and despair over anything ever changing.

Just like physical pain, these pains are not problems themselves but warning signs of deeper issues. We invite you to acknowledge the pain. Stop pretending that everything is okay. Let this pain lead you to discover the root of your brokenness. There are no spiritual anti-inflammatories to relieve this pain, but you can view it as a symptom that will help you diagnose the deeper spiritual struggle. Perhaps your sense of isolation is a symptom of staying so busy that you don't take time to connect with God and others. Bitterness may be a symptom of keeping your focus on what happened in the past rather than focusing on the hope that God offers you for the future. Is your soul weary? Maybe you've been striving too hard to push through all the demands on your life instead of relying on God's Grace. We offer these suggestions not in judgment but as examples of deeper issues that may need healing.

Notice and name your Spiritual pains. Then use The Grace Cycle to move towards healing and Thriving. Don't try to push through this alone. Find others you can trust to walk alongside you, others who are willing to be vulnerable with their own spiritual pain and growth. God has not abandoned you. You can trust, wait, and hope in him to guide you and restore you to Spiritual Wellness.

Practical Suggestions

Spiritual Disciplines offer very helpful, practical tools to experience transformation in this area of your life. When we use the term "disciplines," it may sound like we're asking you to just check off one more to-do list item in your life. We use the term because it's widely used, but we see these as tools to develop habits that can help you experience God's presence in a new way. Three Spiritual Disciplines we find especially helpful in this area are Scripture Meditation, Silence, and Prayer.

Scripture Meditation

I teach a specific meditation process called *Selah* that combines reading scripture passages with the tradition of Centering Prayer. In Centering Prayer (a helpful practice in itself), you quiet your mind and use a word or phrase to help you refocus on silence when your mind wanders.[26] This can be practiced for just a few minutes up to 20 minutes a day. *Selah* meditation begins with reading a short scripture passage (no more than a few verses) and allowing God to highlight one word or phrase. As you quiet your mind for two to seven minutes, you use that word or phrase to bring your mind back to silence and focus as needed.[27] We've used this practice and taught it to many

---

26: A helpful app is *Centering Prayer* from Contemplative Outreach, www.contemplativeoutreach.org

27: My 14 Day Scripture Meditation training is available at a discount here: https://meditation.1fit-wellness.com/

others and find it helps us to move the truths of God's word from our heads into our hearts and souls.

Silence

Silence and Stillness are historical Spiritual Disciplines that are largely forgotten today. We live in such a busy culture that a practice of sitting still and quietly almost feels like punishment, yet our spirits crave this. Taking even a few minutes once or twice a day, even interrupting your busy schedule to sit in Silence, can have surprising benefits. Peter Scazzero writes:

> When you choose to sit in silence and stillness, you are choosing to allow God to be the center of your life. That means you are choosing, even if for just a few moments, to let go of control and your own agenda.
>
> That is no small thing.
>
> But if you persevere through the awkwardness at the beginning—if you truly stop to surrender your will to God's will—you will begin to experience a gradual transformation. And slowly, you will find that silence will become a normal and regular part of each day.[28]

Practicing Silence and Stillness in God's presence has many benefits. The most important is being able to calm your own mind so that you can hear God's voice. When you can silence all the voices in your head that compete for your attention, you can pay closer

---

28: Peter Scazzero, *Emotionally Healthy Spirituality Day by Day* (Grand Rapids, MI: Zondervan, 2018), 14-15

attention to God's direction in your life. It also becomes, as Peter Scazzero says, a part of your daily habits. You become less reactive to stressful situations by pausing before responding. Thoughtful responses begin to replace knee-jerk reactions. Peace begins to rule in your heart, replacing anxious thoughts. You may still have a busy life with a full schedule, but busyness no longer rules your life. And most importantly, you experience the richness of God's presence in your days.

Prayer

If your mind is prone to wander when you attempt Silence or Meditation, then turn to Prayer. You have probably been taught that Prayer is simply having a conversation with God. That is true, but prayer can become as basic as showing God the random things that are on your mind and heart. Sometimes I simply envision holding people before God as they pop into my mind. I may or may not have words, but I know that God knows what they need far better than I do. Prayer can include intercession for others as well as asking God for direction and pausing to listen for answers. Instead of showing God your spiritual "wish list," you can turn prayer into a time of connecting your heart and mind with God's heart and mind.

Questions to Ask in Pursuit of Spiritual Wellness

You might begin to evaluate your Spiritual Wellness by examining your life for the Fruit of the Spirit that Paul described in Galatians 5:22-23. Ask yourself:

- To what degree am I loving others versus living for myself?
- How frequently do I experience joy?
- Is my sense of peace lasting, or does it depend on my circumstances?
- How patient am I? Do I wait on God to work out his plan? Allow others time and space that they need? Am I patient with myself and the transformation I'm seeking?
- To what extent do I extend kindness to others and to myself?
- How much does my life align with and reflect the goodness of God?
- To what degree do I live in integrity and faithfulness, keeping my word to others?
- How much do I project gentleness and understanding in my interactions with others?
- Is my life one that exhibits self-control, or am I driven by my impulses, emotions, and desires?

Also consider:

- What Spiritual Disciplines do I already incorporate in my life?
- What would it look like to add a new Spiritual Discipline?

- What may be getting in the way of experiencing deeper connection to God in my life?

Is there One Simple Change you can make in your life to grow in Spiritual Wellness? Share this with someone you can trust for support and lean into God's Grace for power and transformation in this area.

Spiritual Wellness Case Study

Matt and Amanda prayed day after day, night after night, for the salvation of Matt's father. Matt's dad Arthur was battling metastasized pancreatic cancer, and he wasn't responding well to chemotherapy. Matt and Amanda had met in college through a faith-based campus group. Matt discovered the love of God and chose to follow Jesus through his involvement in the group. While Amanda had grown up in a churchgoing family, Matt was raised by non-religious parents. His dad was particularly hostile toward religions. At their wedding, Arthur grumbled all the way to the church, put on a fake smile for the pictures, and then drank all the way through the reception. He always said, "I don't need any God. I can take care of myself." Whenever Matt brought up the subject of faith and how much God had done for him, Arthur would either change the subject or grunt and turn up the TV.

With Arthur's prospects looking dire, Matt and Amanda found themselves storming the gates of heaven in prayer. Amanda felt this burden especially heavily, not only because she loved her father-in-law, but also because she couldn't bear the thought of telling her children when he died that he probably wouldn't be in heaven. Every time Arthur went in for treatment, she would text him a short "Praying for you!" message, which always went unanswered. She had him on three different prayer chains and frequently told her friends, "We're just trusting that God is going to heal him one way or another—either here on earth or in heaven!" But in her heart, she began to question why God was taking so long to answer their prayers. Arthur's time was running out, so obviously God's time to save him was running out. Did God even care?

One Sunday morning, their pastor preached a sermon about waiting on God from 1 Samuel 13. He showed how Saul had given up on waiting for Samuel to show up and make the sacrifices to God when the enemy surrounding them was much too strong and uncomfortably close. Had Saul waited just one more hour, he would have seen God's deliverance in a powerful way and had his kingdom established. But Saul took control of the situation and offered the sacrifices himself, unwilling to wait any longer. Listening to that sermon, Amanda heard the Holy Spirit prick gently at her heart, asking, "Are you waiting on me, or are you trying to control this situation with Arthur?" As she pondered the message, she began to see that she was trying to get God to do what she wanted by getting as many people as possible on her side in prayer. She was trying to control God! Later that afternoon, she took a long walk and confessed to God that she wasn't trusting him to work in his timing. She admitted that it was really hard to wait because the situation looked so desperate. In that moment, she felt God reassuring her of his love for Arthur, for her, and for her children. She chose to let go of trying to control the outcome and found peace in her heart to replace the desperation she had been living with. Amanda continued to pray for Arthur, but she did so with a renewed trust in God and his plan, even if she couldn't see the good in the moment.

Amanda's experience shows how sometimes that Aha Moment can be sparked by an external prompt (her pastor's sermon) rather than an internal realization (as we illustrated in Bess's story). She took that realization to God and needed to shift her focus from control to acceptance of what she couldn't control. God poured out Grace and love to enable Amanda to let go. While her shift seems simple and small, it profoundly affected her relationship with God and how she prayed. She chose trust over control, and that brought her the peace she thought she could only find if things turned out the way she wanted.

Mental Wellness

Let's begin by distinguishing between "Mental Health" and a Biblical perspective of "Mental Wellness." Both can be seen on a continuum from unhealthy to healthy. Mental Health encompasses "our emotional, psychological, and social well-being. It affects how we think, feel, and act. It also helps determine how we handle stress, relate to others, and make choices."[29] For our purposes here, we recognize that Mental Wellness incorporates all these things and must, from a Biblical standpoint, also include Wisdom. We define Wisdom as "living according to God's values." When we read the Book of Proverbs, we see this laid out clearly: the foolish person follows their own desires and human understanding while the wise person follows God's leading, teaching, and design for life. We spoke earlier of "Goodness," or alignment with God's word, being like the GPS that points towards a life of Wellness. In that sense, Thriving in this area, just as with all the areas we address in this book, goes beyond being "healthy" to being aligned with God's design for your life.

Let's look at a couple of important scripture passages that help us frame this concept of Mental Wellness from a Biblical perspective.

> For though we live in the world, we do not wage war as the world does. The weapons we fight with are not the weapons of the world. On the contrary, they have divine power to demolish strongholds. We demolish arguments

---

29: "What Is Mental Health?" *SAMHSA.Gov*, SAMHSA, www.mentalhealth.gov/basics/what-is-mental-health. Accessed 25 July 2022.

and every pretension that sets itself up against the knowledge of God, and we take captive every thought to make it obedient to Christ (2 Corinthians 10:3-5).

But the wisdom that comes from heaven is first of all pure; then peace-loving, considerate, submissive, full of mercy and good fruit, impartial and sincere (James 3:17).

Our minds can harbor strongholds in the form of arguments and pretensions that deny God. Consider what it means when you allow your imagination to run away and spin out of control. Or when you determine the necessary outcome of a situation and do all you can to control the outcome. Or you believe false messages that have been drilled into your mind for years, messages that may have come from others. You may know they're not true, but you can still live in captivity to those messages. For example, I was bullied in early elementary school. As a result, I carried in my mind the message "no one likes me or wants to be my friend." It's not true, but it was something I needed to battle, a thought that I still need to constantly take captive and surrender to Christ. All of these mental strongholds—living in imaginations, holding on to control of situations, and believing false messages—are opposed to God and the love and freedom he offers you. It is essential to identify your thoughts that are keeping you from living in healthy Connection to God and surrender those thoughts to Christ.

In contrast, there is godly wisdom that James describes. Rather than thoughts, imaginations, and lies that are set up against the knowledge of God and his work in our lives, this wisdom begins with purity. Thoughts filtered through the truth of God's word and connection to the Holy Spirit create peace. That peaceful wisdom shows up in actions: consideration of others, submission to authority, mercy, impartiality, and honesty. Such thinking is humble, surrendered to God, and clear. In contrast, thinking that is ruled by strongholds is unclear, self-focused, and opposed to God's work in your life.

How can you take these unhealthy thoughts captive? How do you destroy the strongholds in your thinking? This is not an earthly battle. The enemy would like nothing more than to knock you into a stronghold of your mind and let you get lost in the labyrinth of your tangled thoughts, thus making you utterly ineffective for Christ and damaging your trust in him. You need to battle for your mind in partnership with the Holy Spirit, seeking God's Grace for transformation. Begin by being aware of your thoughts, slowing down, and pausing to ask if something you believe or are hearing in your mind is true. You need others in your life who can help when you get caught up in cycles of unhealthy thoughts—whether a spouse or a close friend, a small group or a counselor—we all need others to ask us questions such as "Where is this coming from? What message are you believing? Is this really true about you/the situation you're in?" If nothing else, remain in connection with God and journal prayerfully, allowing God to show you the truth about your thoughts.

With that in mind, let's take a look at three principles of Mental Wellness.

Principles of Mental Wellness

Mental Wellness is having a mind aligned to the knowledge of God concerning Him, yourself, and others.

As we saw above in 2 Corinthians 10:5, your thoughts need to be brought into obedience to Christ. Thriving in this area looks like believing the truth and rejecting lies about yourself, about others, and even about God. Still, changing your beliefs is not as simple as just changing what you say, whether out loud or to yourself. Adjusting your internal self-talk is important but only part of the solution. The words you say reflect your deeply held beliefs. Begin by paying attention to your words. Simply observe without judgment what you say to yourself and to others.

Once you have observed your thought and belief patterns, then begin to take those thoughts captive. You might memorize and meditate on scriptures related to themes you have identified. For example, perhaps you recognize you have come to believe you are unworthy of God's love and blessings. Some scriptures that address this and show it to be a lie include 1 John 3:1, 1 Peter 1:18-19, and Colossians 1:12-14. All of these scriptures show how much God loves and treasures you and has chosen you to be his child and inherit his blessings. You could practice internalizing these scriptures and telling yourself these truths to begin to replace the lie you have believed.

You may also begin to identify some of your false beliefs that stem from trauma or negative messages that you internalized as a young age due to traumatic circumstances or wounding words from others. You may need to engage help from a counselor who can help you reframe your mindset to conform with God's truth. Another option might be to participate in body movement or a drama-based therapeutic environment. These have been shown to be powerful in helping people take their thoughts captive to Christ and God's truth.[30]

Wisdom is discerning and choosing the best in any situation in accordance with God's character and will.

Consider the entire Book of Proverbs. Yes, it's about wisdom, yet where does it begin? "The fear of the Lord is the beginning of knowledge" (Proverbs 1:7a). "For the Lord gives wisdom; from his mouth come knowledge and understanding" (Proverbs 2:6). "Trust in the Lord with all your heart and lean not on your own understanding; in all your ways submit to him, and he will make your paths straight. Do not be wise in your own eyes; fear the Lord and shun evil" (Proverbs 3:5-7). Wisdom is living according to God's values because you acknowledge his power, his character, and his majesty. Wisdom is choosing to submit your choices to his direction. And in situations where there is no clear direction from the scriptures, we are told, "If any of you lacks wisdom, you should ask God, who gives generously to all without finding fault, and it will be given to you" (James 1:5). Seek wisdom by seeking to live according to what his word teaches is good. When the path is unclear, ask him.

30: For more about trauma, its impact on our minds and bodies and helpful ways to overcome and reframe mindset, we highly recommend *The Body Keeps the Score* by Bessel A. van der Kolk.

Mental Wellness comes from connection to God by faith in Christ Jesus in the power of the Spirit.

God has created your mind and understands how it is meant to work *and* how it actually works. He sees the strongholds, the wounds, and any limitations in how your mind functions. We say this not in a spirit of judgment but to acknowledge that we live in a fallen world and all have experiences that limit us from fully Thriving in our minds and mindsets. Yet seeking deeper Connection to God, building gratitude, learning to trust and release to him, and tapping into His Grace can help you. Remain in Connection with Jesus (John 15, as we discussed in the previous section) so that you will produce fruit in your mind as well as other areas of your life.

The power of the Holy Spirit through God's Grace is the resource for change in this area. Power is simply the ability to make change happen. We see that in many ways in the world: burning oil creates heat, effective communication may persuade or lead to better understanding, and making choices in line with God's values creates wisdom. Remember that God does not call you to "push through" hard things such as mindset changes. Instead, he offers you his hand to walk into a new direction. He will direct you and empower you as you seek to live wisely in Connection with him.

Using Mental Pain to Identify Areas of Need

Some kinds of mental pain are easy to spot: self-loathing, uncontrollable fear and anxiety, depression, and destructive habits that we hate all fall into that category. Others are much easier to spot in others than in ourselves: harsh judgment, hypocrisy, and narcissistic pride, for example. Still others often lie buried and unnamed: shame and stubbornness. Yet again, these mental pains are not the problem but the symptoms. Learn to pay attention and name them. Let the uncomfortable inconsistency between your thoughts or actions and what you believe to be right call your attention to your true inner thinking. Listening to your pain may lead you to seek therapy to dig up and remove the sting of past hurts that you cling to in order to avoid responsibility. Or it may lead you to build better habits of rest, meditation, and renewal. Avoid self-condemnation and allow this pain as your teacher to lead you to uncover the brokenness beneath.

After delivering the Sermon on the Mount, arguably the most powerful sermon in history (Matthew 5-7), Jesus shared the famous parable of the two foundations. In it he declared that anyone who hears (and presumably understands) His word but doesn't *do* it is like a foolish man who built his house on sand. When the storms of life inevitably come, that person's house (life) will fall into shambles. It is the person who *does* what Jesus says who can be called a wise one who builds their home on a secure foundation of stone. When the storms of life inevitably and inexorably come, that person's life stands firm! So be aware that your actions and fruit say more about your internal beliefs and Mental Wellness than your self-talk does.

Practical Suggestions

Awareness of your mental state is the first and most crucial step towards growth in this area. With this in mind, we recommend three practical elements: journaling, safe community, and therapeutic support.

Journaling

Earlier we suggested an exercise in paying attention and becoming aware of how you speak, especially in your self-talk. Journaling is a great way to identify and begin to change these habits. You might take time at the end of each day to reflect on your thoughts and words and then write some notes in a journal. It doesn't have to be a long entry—just a few notes about what you noticed in your day is enough. Remember not to judge yourself; simply observe and reflect on this. You might ask, "Is it true? Does this align with what God says about me, about others, or about himself?" Identify areas where you may need to shift your beliefs and thoughts. Over time as you choose to change your internal self-talk to align with what God says is true, review what you've written in your journal. You will probably be surprised at the changes you wouldn't notice otherwise.

Journaling can be helpful in many areas, not just in self-talk. We chose self-talk because it's an important shift to make in your Mental Wellness. However, you can journal about many things. The practice of becoming aware and writing down your thoughts is very helpful in transformation. Your journal doesn't have to look like a fifth-grade composition book with neatly-written paragraphs. Maybe it does, but maybe it's random thoughts scattered on a page connected with lines or circles. Drawing and doodling might be a better way for you to journal. Remember to make this practice one that helps you as a unique individual!

Safe Community

We have talked about the importance of Connection with others, and this is one area where that Connection is truly valuable. It is essential to have people in your life you can trust to support your Mental Wellness. We all need people who we can share our struggles with and know we will not receive judgment in response. We also need those people to challenge any unhealthy thinking and point us to the truth. Find your safe community, and if this is a struggle, you are welcome to reach out to us for support in this area.

Therapeutic Support

Sometimes we need more than our own Curiosity and Community to grow and overcome mental blocks and strongholds. There is no shame whatsoever in seeing a therapist or using medication to help you. Be aware that "therapy" can take more forms than simply meeting with a counselor. For some people "talk therapy" works well and helps them to process and reframe their thinking. But it doesn't work for everyone. Give yourself permission to try different therapeutic modalities. You do not need to continue seeing a specific counselor or therapist simply because you've been seeing them for a week, a month, or several years. Use your Curiosity to try something new and reflect on whether it truly helps you. Continue to seek God's direction through your Connection with him and trust him to show you people and resources to grow in Mental Wellness.

Questions to Ask in Pursuit of Mental Wellness

- What do I believe about myself and who I am? Does this align with what God says about me in his word?
- What "strongholds" in my mind are keeping me from living in the truth?
- Am I judging myself for my limiting beliefs or for not producing fruit that I expect in my life? What does God say about me and my life right now?
- What Scriptures can I meditate on to bring my thinking into alignment with God's truth?
- Who are the safe people in my life I can trust to recognize when I am falling captive to lies and who will speak truth to me?
- Would it be wise for me to pursue some kind of professional or therapeutic support in this area?

Mental Wellness Case Study

Elsa couldn't fall asleep. On the rare occasion when she found herself so exhausted that she could barely stay awake, she woke up two hours later with her mind spinning. Fears and "what ifs" about the future battled alongside regrets about things she had said or done in the previous days to keep her from sleep. Most nights she moved out to the sofa in her living room so she wouldn't wake her husband. She scrolled through Facebook for hours to distract her mind from all the anxieties until she finally passed out in exhaustion, dropping the phone on the floor.

She finally talked to her doctor who prescribed her medication for sleep under the condition that she speak with a therapist about the anxious thoughts that were keeping her from sleep. He warned her that while she might be able to sleep with the medication, the worries that were keeping her awake at night would not go away on their own. Reluctantly, Elsa showed up at the first counseling appointment feeling like she must have failed miserably at life to end up needing this level of help.

Yet the counselor helped her far more than she realized. Over the course of the first few sessions, she taught Elsa some breath and meditation techniques to help her calm her mind whenever the worries came up. Then a few weeks into their sessions together, the therapist began to ask some questions about Elsa's family growing up. Memories she had long buried slowly bubbled to the surface: nights of waking up to the sound of her parents arguing, often followed by the slam of the door as her father stormed out. Then she would hear her mother sobbing miserably and sometimes hear the front door open and shut as her mother left the house to chase her dad down. Left alone in her home as a small child, Elsa would curl up and imagine all the bad things that could happen with no one there to protect her.

It was no wonder that nighttime, particularly bedtime, brought up so much worry and fear for Elsa. She had learned at a very young age that she was not safe in bed at night. Whether she was left alone in the house or not, scary things happened then. After some time in therapy and with EMDR treatment, Elsa was able to dissociate from the fears that surrounded sleeping and finally find rest at night. She had filled the prescription from her doctor once, but she ended up not needing it long-term.

Elsa's story demonstrates a simple connection between mental un-wellness and past trauma. But even simple connections aren't always obvious. In her case, professionals (her doctor and therapist) needed to guide her to discover the underlying root of her pain. God in his Grace often uses unexpected people to help us find the path to Wellness. Elsa's story also demonstrates embracing Acceptance of the past that she couldn't change in order to move into a new future. Finally, she tried more than One Simple Change. She believed that medication to help her sleep would solve her problem, but in the end, therapeutic support to uncover and process the wounds from her past led her to healing.

Emotional Wellness

In her groundbreaking work on human experience and emotions, *Atlas of the Heart*, Brené Brown shares that in her research, most people are only aware in the moment of experiencing a very limited range of emotions: happiness, sadness, and   anger.[31] Yet her book addresses a range of 87 experiences and emotions, which she narrowed down from well over a hundred. This illustrates how much we as a culture have trained ourselves to ignore our emotions. Yet God created us to be emotional beings. Our emotions are in part a reflection of his character, his image in us. And in part, our emotions—when we pay attention to them—can help us engage more fully in life. They can act as thermometers, helping us to understand how our environment or relationships are impacting us. Choosing to be aware of your emotions may be uncomfortable, but it becomes one of the best ways to understand yourself.

Consider the range of emotions Jesus demonstrated in his life on earth:

He experienced sadness and deep grief. When his dear friend Lazarus lay dead, he wept (John 11:45). He expressed sorrow over his people not recognizing him as Messiah and the dire consequences they would suffer as a result (Matthew 23:37-39). In the Garden of Gethsemane, we see him in grief and anguish, beseeching the Father three times to make another way to avoid the intense suffering that

---

31: Brown, Brené *Atlas of the Heart: Mapping Meaningful Connection and the Language of Human Experience*. Kindle edition. Random House Publishing Group, 2021, Introduction. loc 218.

lay before him (Matthew 26:36-44). He asked his closest friends to stay awake and pray with him, telling them, "My soul is overwhelmed with sorrow to the point of death" (Matthew 26:38). He felt disappointment when they slept instead of supporting him in prayer.

He felt anger. Passionate anger. When he walked into the temple and saw merchants overcharging and extorting the people who came to offer sacrifices, he responded in a way that people today would consider "losing it." But Jesus remained in control of his anger, even in driving out the merchants and money changers (John 2:14-17). He frequently confronted the Pharisees for leading the people away from God with the laws they had created to control the people's behavior (Matthew 23:1-36).

On the cross and in the hours leading to his crucifixion, he experienced shame. Even though the shame placed on him had nothing to do with his own actions, he felt it. He was subjected to abusive mocking and relentless torment while stripped naked and exposed to the world. The accounts we read in the Bible only give us a hint of the shame he suffered.

And while the Gospels don't clearly spell this out, we can be sure he experienced joy and happiness often. How could he not as he enjoyed friendship with his disciples? When he freed people from diseases and demons that had held them captive for years, sometimes decades? When he saw people finally understand that he was more than a teacher but the Messiah they had longed to see? Even at the Last Supper, Jesus spoke with affection and joy to his disciples, calling them his friends.

Seeing these emotions in Jesus's life shows us that God created us to experience a full range of emotions. We are, after all, created in

God's image. Jesus's humanity does not mean that he was made to be like us. Rather, his life demonstrates a perfect experience of humanity as God intended. If you need more evidence that God accepts and honors all of our emotions, look at the Psalms. David and the other Psalmists use raw language to express their emotions: anger, sadness, fear, grief, anguish, and shame as well as joy, connection, worth, and much more. Laments are valued as highly as praise. Fear is just as important as trust.

When we don't allow ourselves to fully feel and lean into *every* emotion, even those we consider "negative" or "difficult," we significantly limit our experience as humans. Nowhere in the scriptures do we see a healthy or commendable example of a person numbing their feelings, yet that is exactly what we do much of the time. Grief feels too heavy, so we turn to the pantry for "comfort." When shame is unbearable, we turn to alcohol, social media, or other addictive behaviors so we don't have to face it. And fear? We've devalued and degraded this emotion because we don't know how to handle it in a healthy way—so we attribute it to attacks from Satan or tell ourselves that if we speak of our fears, we're bound to have the thing we fear happen. (Raise your hand if you, like me, were raised with "don't speak it into existence" teaching.) We live as though happiness and joy are the only good and healthy emotions, so we try to avoid and cover all other emotions. This is not life! God shows us throughout the Bible that he intends for us to feel emotions and to use those feelings to grow.

There are two important lessons to learn here. First, learn to accept and feel your feelings and emotions, even when they're inconvenient or unbearably uncomfortable. Growth occurs through the process of experiencing what is difficult and learning to live through it. Remember that you are not alone—God is with you, and he brings others to support you. Denying, hiding, or numbing your emotions never creates peace. In fact, it creates the opposite—striving and stuffing as counterfeits for true peace.

Second, it's helpful to consider why you feel what you feel. My wise friend Elizabeth shared that when she has strong emotions over something, she needs to ask herself what is underneath it. Is the feeling really due to the situation that immediately triggered it, or is it connected to another experience? She likes to say, "If you didn't have this feeling, you wouldn't know there is something that needs to be dealt with." Another way to put it is to see your emotions not as the pilot of your life, taking you where they want to go, but like the map.[32] They help you understand where you are, how you got here, and how to navigate to where you want to be. If you let your emotions drive your life, they will take you unpredictably to places you may not want to go, possibly damaging relationships and your mental and spiritual state. However, if you see your emotions as the map or compass, they can help you discover a new route towards Wellness.

32: This helpful map metaphor is from Brown, Brené *Atlas of the Heart*. Kindle edition. Random House Publishing Group, 2021, Introduction.

Principles of Emotional Wellness

Emotional Wellness is benefiting from the full range of human emotions being restored to their sinless beauty.

Our emotions, particularly our difficult emotions, can help us become aware of our experiences and move towards a more healthy life. However, it is important to note that emotions themselves are rooted in God's image in us. We were not given emotions as a result of the fall. If that were the case, Jesus would never have exhibited anger (Matthew 21:12-14), sadness (John 11:33-36), even despair and fear (Mark 26:32-39). We can certainly expect an eternity of full, unrequited joy in God's presence with no more need for grief or sadness (Isaiah 25:6-9; Revelation 21:4). And yet in this life, we can experience a full range of emotions in a healthy way. You may be angry, then pause to understand what lies beneath the anger. The anger may lead you to pursue reconciliation or act to correct injustice rather than causing harm to others. In sadness, you can learn to be tender with yourself and others. If you open up the causes of your sadness in connection with others, you can build deeper relationships. Exploring fears may lead to correcting your actions to live more wisely. Or they may lead you to surrender to God and move out of your comfort zone. Even shame can have a healthy expression; it can lead to repentance or to vulnerability and connection with others.

When you learn to live with your emotions, neither denying them nor allowing them to rule and drive your life, you experience freedom and Thrive in a fresh way!

Emotional Wellness comes from vulnerability
with God and trust in His goodness.

We wrote earlier about "Mutual Delight" with God, loving God, and fully experiencing his love. This is truly a vulnerable experience. God seeks for you to come to him with all that you are. Again, if you spend much time reading the Psalms, you see people pouring their hearts out openly and honestly to God. He holds no judgment for his children in this! When Jesus walked on the earth, he reserved his judgment for the Pharisees and teachers who tried to hide their humanity from God and others, not for people who came to him in sorrow and desperation. God does not expect perfection from you. He longs for you to bring your whole self, even your brokenness and questions, to him. When you discover his loving acceptance for you as you are right now, then you can bring all of your emotions to him. Trust him. He is good and loving!

Emotional Wellness comes from Connection to God by
faith in Jesus in the power of the Spirit.

You can experience transformation in this area by surrendering to Christ. Recognize and admit any brokenness you have in this area. What emotions tend to run away with you? What emotions do you try to run from? The first step to transformation is to become Curious about your experience, and emotions are one of the best gifts God has given us to engage Curiosity.

Invite God into your emotions. Embrace who he made you to be, even your emotions. Remember that emotions are a part of his image in you. You might explore the Psalms or the life of Jesus to see how others in the Bible have expressed emotions that you are familiar with. Admit to God how you over- or under-express your emotions and seek out how you can grow in just one.

Finally, ask God for help in guarding your heart (Proverbs 4:23). In 2 Thessalonians 3:5, Paul wrote, "May the Lord direct your hearts into God's love and Christ's perseverance." God's love can guide you to guard against a hard heart while the example of Christ's perseverance can build courage and help you guard against a faint heart.[33]

Noticing the joys in your life might lead you to build new family habits of time together. It might lead you into community with others walking with God. And celebrating joy will almost certainly steal the pain and isolation that comes from emotional brokenness. So let your joys also become your teachers and use Curiosity, Connection, and Grace to move toward increased health and Emotional Wellness.

Using Joy to Point You to Emotional Health

Much of this section has been about recognizing, naming, and learning from your painful feelings. So let's turn this one around. Many of us are far more aware of our painful emotions than our positive ones. If you are not currently in the throes of a beautiful romance, anticipating a new family member, beginning an exciting new stage of life, or celebrating a big success, chances are that you are living on "autopilot" unless pain grabs your attention. You can pay attention to and name moments of happiness, contentment, peace,

---

33: See Karen's teaching "Heart Wholeness" at His Shelter Church for more on this: https://youtu.be/ZR5cSGKUNVs

love, and joy when you experience them. As you become aware of these emotions, let them become your teachers pointing you towards Emotional Wellness. Thriving isn't so much about moving away from our brokenness but rather about moving toward experiencing God's goodness and love. So allow yourself to notice and rest in God's goodness and love. This doesn't mean that Emotional Wellness looks like being joyful and happy all the time. However, when you experience all of your emotions that stem from your identity as a beloved child of God, then you truly Thrive.

Practical Suggestions

Some of us experience our emotions very deeply, even to the point where we let our feelings drive our actions without thinking. Others are not very engaged with emotions to the point where they may be mostly unaware of their feelings. Whether you tend to over-express or under-express your emotions, or fall somewhere in the middle, here are some helpful suggestions to help you Thrive in this area:

Check in with your Emotions

If you're a typical person who is only aware of feeling sad, angry, or happy, then your first step can be to expand your emotional vocabulary. An Emotion Wheel (or Feelings Wheel) can provide a good place to begin.[34] Start by looking at the wheel and become aware

---

34: Many Emotions Wheels are available on the internet. One that has a helpful emotional vocabulary is at https://www.calm.com/blog/the-feelings-wheel, but you can download one from any of a number of websites.

of the wide range of emotions available to you. Then you can move a little deeper in awareness by checking in with your emotional state once a day. If you need to, set an alarm on your phone and simply stop to ask, "What emotion am I experiencing right now?" (Don't worry about whether you are able to check in with every emotion throughout your day, just do this a few times.) You might begin with the most general emotions named at the center of the wheel, and as you become more familiar with this, move further out to distinguish more specific emotions. Avoid judging your emotions as you check in with yourself.

Sensory Grounding

This technique may help you return to a more balanced state if you feel flooded with an emotion and are struggling to control it. Simply pause, become aware of your immediate surroundings, and name:

5 things you can see
4 things you can touch
3 things you can hear
2 things you can smell
1 thing you can taste

This is a helpful way to return to a more stable state so that you can deal with whatever triggered the strong emotional response.

Meditation and Breath Work

Earlier we talked about the value of Scripture Meditation and Silence in God's presence to build your Spiritual Wellness. These practices are also helpful in training your nervous system to respond in a more balanced way rather than being emotionally overwhelmed. Breathing techniques are also helpful. When you are in a calm place, practice "Balanced Breathing" by inhaling and exhaling for the same amount of time, such as a count of Four for each inhale and exhale. Repeat up to 10 times. When you experience strong emotions, you can use this breathing practice to help your mind and body become more calm. The point is not to avoid experiencing the emotion but to help your mind and body calm down so that you can choose how to respond appropriately in the moment.

Questions to Ask in Pursuit of Emotional Wellness

- What emotions are you aware of experiencing on a typical day?
- When do you tend to experience anger? Does your anger arise out of sadness, fear, betrayal, or loss of control? When was the last time you felt angry? What triggered that anger?
- When did you last cry? Is sadness a normal emotion or one you avoid? What does this tell you about yourself?
- What are you afraid of? (Become aware of your fears without judging whether they are realistic or not.)

- When do you experience joy, happiness, or delight? How can you cultivate more of this in your life?
- Are there other emotions that drive you, that you are driven to experience, or that you avoid?
- What else has this chapter brought to mind in relation to your Emotional Wellness?

Emotional Wellness Case Study

Hallie lost it with her seven-year-old again. Of course it was over the stupidest little thing, but really, how many times should she have to ask her son to put his shoes in the closet when he walked in the door instead of kicking them across the kitchen and leaving them there? After she snapped at him, he sheepishly picked up his shoes and put them away, but she felt guilty for her reaction. And she continued to feel on edge for the rest of the evening until bedtime. When her 12 -year-old daughter asked yet again to watch YouTube videos before finishing her homework, Hallie used her best "I'm rolling my eyes at you on the inside" voice to remind her of the rule of no TV before finishing homework. When her husband walked in the door and tried to give her a hug as she was standing in front of the stove cooking, she shrugged him off. She sat silently through dinner, stewing inside. The worst part was that she knew this happened far more often than she liked. She wanted to show up understanding and patient for her kids, but it seemed like the after-school drama and chaos always set her off. She knew something needed to change, but what?

Hallie's best friend Jess seemed like the most patient saint on the planet, always kind and understanding, even when her kids were acting like... well, children. One day when they were having coffee together, Hallie took a risk to share what had been going on at home. She said, "You just always have it together with your kids. How do you do it?" Rather than just spilling her "secret" to being patient, Jess took time to ask Hallie some questions. Was she likely to lose it on certain days more than others? How was she sleeping at night? Did she make a point of having balanced meals while the kids were at school? Her questions helped Hallie to realize that she wasn't being a "bad mom." She was physically and emotionally drained by the time she picked the kids up from school. She had a habit of scheduling appointments right up until it was time to leave. She often skipped lunch, and she tended to sleep late on the weekends to make up for not getting enough sleep during the week. By Wednesday and Thursday most weeks, her emotional resources had been depleted, and she had no patience for anything. It wasn't so much that the kids were misbehaving on those days more than others—she just didn't have the energy to hold things together any longer.

Hallie began building a new habit of taking a 10 to 20 minute break to rest before she left to pick up the kids after school. Even if she couldn't control much of the rest of her schedule during the day, she found she was able to make that one small adjustment. After a few weeks, she found she felt much better and happy to see her kids at the end of their day. Rather than snapping at and berating her son about his shoes, she gently reminded him and with humor warned him that if he didn't put them away, she would hide them from him. She had a conversation with her daughter where they made some agreements about TV and schoolwork, and she released her daughter to take responsibility for getting her work done. She began to greet her husband warmly when he came home, and overall, she felt much more peace in her life.

Hallie's story shows the power of One Simple Change to create a shift in her life. She also made a point of connecting with a trusted friend to help her uncover the root of her struggle. Her friend helped her use Curiosity to discover the root issue instead of trying to tell her what she needed to change. Jess recognized that Hallie's struggles were unique to her, and the way that Jess managed her emotions wouldn't necessarily help Hallie.

CHAPTER 6

The Connecting Three:
How I Relate to My World

"Whatever you do, whether in word or deed,
do it all in the name of the Lord Jesus, giving
thanks to God the Father through him."

Colossians 3:17

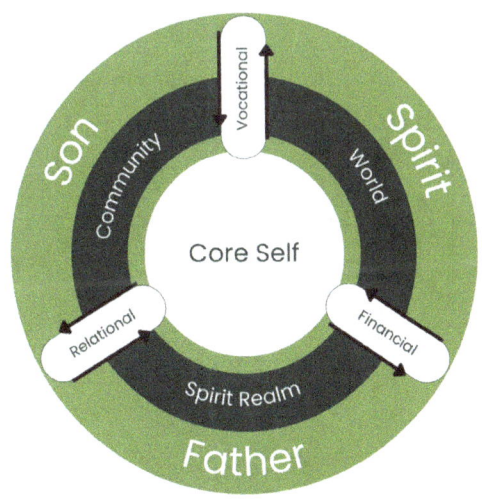

Relational Wellness

Even after more than 22 years of marriage, Allie and John struggled to communicate their needs to one another. Allie's work involved a few weeks each year when she had high demands on her time and energy. John had learned over the years that during those seasons, she needed him to take over more of the household tasks and give her some space. Allie appreciated him giving her this space—until she noticed that about six weeks after her busy season had ended, her husband was still physically and emotionally distant. John tended to be more of the "touchy-feely" type of the two of them, so Allie began to question his ongoing distance. Was she no longer attractive to him? Had her weight gain of the last year or so turned his attention elsewhere? Did he still want her for a wife? After a few days of stewing, she found the courage to ask her husband what was going on. Other than, "Well, I know you've been busy with work," he didn't have much else to say.

She immediately reacted by shutting down the conversation. "Thanks, good talk," she said and walked away. This led to an argument over their expectations of one another, but eventually, they were able to listen to one another and reach a better understanding of each other's needs and expectations around intimacy in their marriage.

In their relationship, Allie and John each had expectations of the other, of their interactions, and of their own selves. But they hadn't fully communicated these expectations to one another. And because of those underlying expectations, they began telling themselves stories about why the other wasn't acting as hoped. It took an open, honest conversation where they both shared about those expectations in order to resolve the conflict.

As I look at my own relationships and observe others, I've seen that our interactions with others can be improved or broken by our perspective. This perspective is nearly always influenced by past relationships, often from our earliest years. Can you think of a conflict with another person that you've had recently? What happened (whether something was said out loud or not) that may have touched on pain from your past? In the beginning of this book, I shared a conflict that Michael and I had that brought up for me messages from my early childhood. He didn't intend to communicate these things to me, but in his actions, I heard "you're too much for me" and "what you have to say doesn't matter." These messages came from inside me, not from him. I needed to look at how that incident played out as a mirror reflecting my own heart so that I could discover what needed to change inside of me in order to improve our relationship.

At the same time, Michael needed to discover how his response impacted me, but I was only responsible for myself. This is a critical element to adopt in Relational Wellness: awareness that the only person I have any control over is myself. I cannot control any other person. I cannot get them to say or do the things I want, expect or need them to say or do, even if I communicate my desires. Let me repeat that. *Even if I clearly communicate my desires*, it won't necessarily get me the response I hope for. Admittedly, manipulative tactics can work to a certain extent, but in the end they will fall short and seriously damage or break the relationship.

In Romans 12:18, Paul wrote, "If it is possible, as far as it depends on you, live at peace with everyone." The context of this verse is about being kind to enemies and not taking revenge when hurt (verses 17-21). This reinforces the importance of taking responsibility for my part in maintaining peace with others. You may not be able to stop harmful or evil words or actions towards you, but you can choose your response. You can choose peace and kindness over returning wounding words or vengeful actions. You can choose to hold boundaries or not. You can choose to withdraw or fight or seek a middle ground. It's not always (ever?) easy, but as in all things, it is worth pushing through the difficulty and pain to achieve growth.

Principles of Relational Wellness

Relational Wellness is being in relationships of mutual delight and service with God and others.

This theme runs through the entire Bible. God's original design for Adam and Eve was that they serve him together as managers of his creation. God planned for them to do this in a state of intimate connection with him, walking and talking with him daily. God intended for them to love and serve him and one another, delighting in all that he had made. Sadly, this ended with their fall into disobedience and sin. But even after the fall, we see God making space repeatedly for people to come to him and experience his love. In the Tabernacle and later the Temple, God brought his presence to the Ark of the Covenant. This Ark was far more than a holy box. It served as the place where his people were reminded of his covenant of love with them. Even more, it was the place where they could come to him to find mercy. The top of the Ark was called the "Mercy Seat," a reminder that God would meet his people and offer them mercy. Later in history, Jesus came to earth as Immanuel, God with us! God came to live among us humans, bringing mercy, forgiveness, compassion, correction, and direction. Furthermore, the letters of Paul and Peter speak often of our role as Christ's body, such that each of us brings something needed to express God's presence on earth.

We serve God, our community, and our world together. We need one another, and we are called to service through acts of love for God and one another. Of course our relationships can get messy. But when we pursue Wellness and the life that God has designed for us, we work through these difficulties and find great rewards and blessings as a result.

Relational Wellness includes speaking truth in love.

The phrase "speaking the truth in love" from Ephesians 4:15 is often used by Christians in ways that Paul did not intend. The context (verses 13-16) is about being built up in maturity as the Body of Christ. It is not about confronting sin in others—it is most certainly *not* about confronting sin in the world outside of the church. Instead, "speaking the truth in love" means truthful teaching that is based in love for one another with the goal of unity in the church. With grace we teach, encourage, and even rebuke one another when necessary, but we *always* do so with the goal of maturity and unity. Our goal is never to put ourselves above others (see Philippians 2) but to gently lift one another up and point one another to Christ. Sometimes we need to work through anger with one another, remembering the goal is always restoration and unity. When speaking to others, remember Paul's words: "Let your speech always be with grace, as though seasoned with salt, so that you will know how you should respond to each person" (Colossians 4:6).

Relational Wellness replaces judgment of others
with patient forgiveness.

Jesus spoke of how crucial forgiveness of others is, even saying that if we don't forgive others, we risk not being forgiven by God (Matthew 6:12-16, Matthew 18:21-35)! While his grace is not dependent on our actions, we cannot take this warning lightly. Unforgiveness often stems from judging the intentions of another person. If you remember that you are the only person you are responsible for, the only person whose actions you have any control over, the only person whose feelings are your responsibility, can you really know the thoughts and intentions of another person's heart? It is far better to let go of the burden of what has been done to you by another person, while trusting God who knows all hearts. Trust in him as your loving Father and the judge of all people. Dr. Caroline Leaf writes, "Scientific research shows that forgiveness and love are good for your mind, brain and body health! ...People who develop an ability to forgive have greater control over their emotions; are significantly less angry, upset, and hurt; and are much healthier."[35] When you release to God the burden of others' choices and actions and take responsibility for your own, you are well on your way to a far more peaceful, stable life.

35: Leaf, Caroline. *Think, Learn, Succeed: Understanding and Using Your Mind to Thrive at School*, the Workplace, and Life. Baker Books, 2019, p. 70.

Using Relational Pain to Identify Areas of Need

This is a little more challenging than other areas because relationships require more than one person. An area of pain and struggle usually arises because both people in the relationship have failed to engage in a healthy way. This can lead to symptoms such as ongoing conflict over a specific issue, unforgiveness and resentment, hiding true feelings, or disengaging from the relationship. When you identify an area that is causing discord in a relationship, look below the surface. Do you need to address a physical, spiritual, mental, or emotional struggle? Or do you have elements in your past that are invading a current relationship—your pain may not be about the other person in your difficult relationship but about how their interactions with you reflect a painful part of your story. Open communication, while risky, is the key to healing in relationships.

Conflict in itself is not a symptom of a problem in a relationship. You may have grown up in a family where conflict was always swept under the rug, or your past may involve ugly arguments with blaming and shaming others. Neither extreme is healthy. Yet conflict, when addressed in a healthy way, is a powerful step towards growth in a relationship. If you have a relationship characterized by frequent fights, take time to learn how to fight fair.[36] Take ownership of your own feelings and actions, and when you do need to confront

---

36: For a host of tools in building healthy relationships and learning to fight fair, we recommend Scazzero, Peter, and Geri Scazzero. *Emotionally Healthy Relationships: Discipleship That Deeply Changes Your Relationship with Others*. HarperCollins Christian Publishing, 2021.

another person, do so in love with the goal of building unity in your relationship.

Practical Suggestions

A key scripture for our relationships is Jesus's words in John 13:34-35: "A new commandment I give to you, that you love one another, even as I have loved you, that you also love one another. By this all men will know that you are my disciples, if you have love for one another." Jesus also told us, "Do to others as you would have them do to you" (Luke 6:31). Loving one another because of his love and simply practicing this "Golden Rule" form the basis of how we experience Relational Wellness.

Any discussion of loving others would be incomplete without looking at 1 Corinthians 13:4-7. Consider this a filter for how you interact with others:

> Love is patient, love is kind. It does not envy, it does not boast, it is not proud. It does not dishonor others, it is not self-seeking, it is not easily angered, it keeps no record of wrongs. Love does not delight in evil but rejoices with the truth. It always protects, always trusts, always hopes, always perseveres.

As you read this list, pay attention to where you struggle. Being patient? Honoring others? Being easily angered? Consider why those are struggles for you and pray about One Simple Change in this area. Here are a few practical tips to help in Relational Wellness:

Stop taking responsibility for others' feelings

How often do people say "you made me feel…"? Don't own that. Not only are you the only person you have any amount of control over, but you are the only person whose emotions you can be responsible for. Yes, you may have said or done something that triggered a feeling in them, but unless you intended to wound with your words or actions, you are not responsible for another person's reaction. Live in the truth that your control ends where you end. If you do hurt another person through your words or actions, then apologize and seek reconciliation. But do so by taking responsibility for your own actions and not for the other person's response.

Practice Pausing

Consider the people you know who are most at peace and least anxiety-driven. There's a good chance they are slower in their conversations and responses than most others. Were you ever taught that when you're angry, you should take a breath and count to ten? This simple practice of pausing before responding is powerful. When faced with a situation or words that wound (or bring up old wounds), pause. Breathe. Take a moment to look inside at what emotions are coming up, and then choose your response. Will you get this right every time? Not likely. It takes time and practice to learn. Could you be interrupted or accused of not answering? Possibly. But remember that's not about you—if another person is impatient for your response, their feelings are not your responsibility.

Know that You Are Loved

Jesus could tell us to love one another because he loved us far more deeply than any of us can ever know. When we can approach life being deeply rooted in his love for us, it will impact how we show up in all our relationships. In order to live out of this love, I encourage you to take time each day resting in his loving presence. You don't need to do anything else such as praying or studying the Bible—just sit with Jesus, be quiet, and let him show up for you in love. As an added bonus, practicing this kind of "quiet time" with Jesus for even five to ten minutes a day will help you learn to pause and respond rather than reacting in your interactions with others.

Questions to Ask in Pursuit of Relational Wellness

- Think about some of the "easier" relationships you have with others. What makes those relationships and interactions feel easier?

- Consider your more difficult relationships. What is hard about them? Is there anything in common in these relationships? What can you take responsibility for, and what can you release responsibility for?

- What does "speaking the truth in love" look like in your life? Do you seek to build up others and create unity through your words? Do your words look like 1 Corinthians 13?

- Are you holding on to any judgments or unforgiveness of another person?
- How does your relationship with God influence how you show up in relationships with others?

Relational Wellness Case Study

Kara started telling her friends that she was no longer talking to Janine. Very few of Kara's friends had relationships with one another, so her falling-out with Janine didn't impact anyone else, but her sister Joyce wondered about it and asked Kara what happened. She said that Janine was being judgmental towards Kara's daughter, and she didn't need that in her life. Over time Kara just stopped talking about Janine altogether. Joyce noticed this happened from time to time with Kara and her friends.

When Kara had surgery, Joyce organized a meal train to help Kara's family. One evening, Kara called and asked her to take their friend Robin off the list because she didn't want her coming over any more. Joyce asked what had happened, and Kara confided that Robin and her husband had been flirting with each other when Robin dropped off a meal that afternoon. Knowing Robin well, Joyce couldn't imagine Robin flirting with anyone else's husband. She expected that Kara had misinterpreted the interaction that she observed. After a few more calls and conversations, Joyce convinced Kara to meet with her and Robin together to see if they could straighten out the situation.

When they got together, Kara was cold and distant, clearly not willing to have this conversation at all. Robin was hurt because she had no idea why Kara had suddenly stopped responding to her texts asking about her recovery. Joyce recognized that she couldn't force the two women to be reconciled, yet she also had observed how much they had each gained from their friendship with one another. Patiently, she invited them each to share their perspective on what happened the day that Robin dropped off a meal. Robin was shocked to realize that her friendly banter with Kara's husband had been taken as flirting. She knew that Kara's first husband had cheated on her, so she understood how deeply it would hurt Kara to feel that her current husband might be attracted to another woman. Robin apologized. Kara forgave her. And while the relationship remained strained for some time, they began to restore their friendship. The incident also gave Joyce an opportunity to help Kara look a little more closely at how she reacted when she felt hurt or offended by a friend. Kara began to see that others weren't being malicious towards her and that usually what she took as judgment or criticism was often a miscommunication.

In this story, Kara had been living unaware of how wounds and trauma from her past caused her to see others' behavior as threats. With her sister's patient and understanding support, Kara began to understand how she was reacting by shutting others out of her life. Joyce could speak into Kara's life because Kara trusted her completely. While often messy, relationships with others can lead to significant growth and maturity.

Vocational Wellness

At 50 years old, I finally figured out what I wanted to be! I had worked in a number of different jobs since graduating from college. I started in bookkeeping/accounting and then in administrative/secretarial positions. I ran a nonprofit organization for a few years as well as trying to build businesses through a couple of different network marketing companies. I did well at all of my jobs, largely because my parents had instilled a good work ethic in me as I grew up, but nothing really felt like "me." But when I began to teach group fitness classes and later moved into mentoring others, boom! That work fit me in ways I never could have imagined it would! It brought together many skills I had built over the years (dance, choreography, public speaking) as well as my passion to help others become the best they could be. In the movie *Chariots of Fire*, Eric Liddel says, "When I run, I feel his [God's] pleasure." In the same way, when I step in front of a class, turn on the music, and begin to instruct others in movements, I feel fully alive, as though I'm doing exactly what God made me do.

Feeling fully yourself, alive, and passionate in your work is the ultimate expression of Vocational Wellness. But if you don't feel that, how can you achieve a sense of being fully alive in your work, especially if you're stuck in a job that may pay the bills but doesn't really feel satisfying?

In Ecclesiastes, Solomon wrote, "I know that there is nothing better for people than to be happy and to do good while they live. That each of them may eat and drink, and find satisfaction in all their toil—this is the gift of God" (Ecclesiastes 3:12-13). To find satisfaction in your work is a gift from God. But many people toil away every day in unsatisfying work. If you find yourself in this place, you face a choice to disengage, to push through, or to seek what God has for you. "Quiet Quitting" has become a trend in recent years where burned-out employees disengage from their work by putting in only the minimum required of them. Conversely, you might choose to suck it up and work harder, which might make you look good to your employer but may not benefit you. It can put you at risk for burnout and not necessarily gain any recognition or additional pay just for doing what is expected. So where is the answer?

As in all things, I encourage you to turn to Curiosity to find a solution. Here are a few things you might look at:

- In Genesis 3, we see God's curse on Adam's work. You've probably been taught that this was punishment for their disobedience. We have a different perspective— we believe that God made life harder for humanity so that we would recognize our need for his mercy and turn our attention to him. While we live in a fallen world, our hearts still long for Eden where work always felt purposeful and satisfying. God intends this longing for Eden to draw our hearts back to him. If your work is difficult or challenging, let it help you turn your attention to God and your need for him.
- Maybe your challenges stem from an unhealthy work environment. Can you opt out of any drama and toxicity that surrounds you at work? If this is the case, take some time to talk to God about your role and what you have power to change in your workspace. Remember what we spoke about in the previous section on Relational

Wellness. You only have control over yourself, but there may be things you can change in how you interact with others at work.

- You might need to change your work, whether moving to another company or a different career. We recognize this isn't always easy, but if your work is causing you a level of stress that makes it difficult to show up in healthy ways in the rest of your life, you need to look at why you have chosen to stay in that work.

- One other option is to find your vocation outside of what you do to earn income. Vocational "success" is the intersection of your skills and passions with the needs of the people around you. This produces fruit. Think of "bearing fruit" as not just a spiritual result but the outcome of a life planted and provisioned by God (see Psalm 1 and Jeremiah 17:7-8). Where can you serve God and others in a way that lines up with your personality, passions, and gifts?

In Colossians 1:9-12, Paul prays for God's people to be filled with the knowledge of his will, and he prays for one of the results to be that they will bear fruit in every good work. That is our hope and prayer for you also, that as you pursue the principles we outline here, you will bear fruit and find joy in your service!

Using Vocational Pain to Identify Areas of Need

We just suggested a number of areas where challenges in your work might point you to a need for change. But it is wise to evaluate what lies beneath the difficulty. Does your work feel fruitless because it doesn't suit you well? Would additional training be beneficial—and if so, where can you find it? If you could choose anything different, what would be your ideal vocation? If something about your work environment is painful, take a look at what part you may have in that. Before simply leaving to find another job, seek what God might have for you in the difficulty. When you stretch, you grow!

Principles of Vocational Wellness

Vocational Wellness is working in the world as an expression of your identity as a child of God.

As a child of God and part of the Body of Christ, your role is to partner with God in the work he is doing in the world. Following the leading of the Holy Spirit, seek opportunities to engage in his work. This may look like serving together with other children of God. It need not be serving and working independently. Even if you don't have other followers of Jesus directly alongside you in your labor, invite your faith community to support you in your work through prayer. Identify and step into your calling, whether it's a new calling or a place where you have been working for some time. There is no need to do more or less than your calling. God uses many of his children to accomplish his purposes. Rely on his Grace to empower you in your work.

> *Vocational Wellness is enthusiastically and faithfully embracing God's exquisite design for you and your unique gifts to fulfill God's purposes in the world.*

When you experience Connection to God, you can explore more deeply who He has made you to be and his calling for your life. We mentioned that vocational success begins when your skills and passions intersect with the needs in the world around you. Therefore, in order to Thrive in this area, you start by understanding yourself better: your skills, your passions, how your mind works, even your life experience. These are all parts of how God made you uniquely. When you understand who you truly are, then you can engage in the work that he calls you to, partnering with him as he works in the world.

Embrace the amazing creation God has made in you! While it's a trite saying, it is true that there is only one you in this world and no one else can take your place. Explore how God has uniquely designed you and serve him and others (your family, your community, your employer) in line with your own gifts and purpose.

Transformation occurs when we trust God to provide as we faithfully serve according to his design for us, and as we rest and celebrate with our families.

Thriving in this area of your life requires that you not only discover his design and purpose for you but also rely on his Grace. You may choose to step in faith into a new area of calling. Trust that God is big enough to even use your falls and learning experiences for his purposes in the world. Celebrate with others in your family or faith community when you experience the successes he gives you!

When you work, work diligently, but also take time to rest. We need rest and breaks from our work. Many people who observe a weekly day of rest (or Sabbath, which need not be on a specific day of the week—see Romans 14:5-6a) find that the day off helps them recharge and gain more energy for the next week's work. Jesus said "the Sabbath was made for man" (Mark 2:27a), and while we are using this a little out of its context, it's an important point. God instituted the Sabbath because he knows we need to rest from our work on a regular basis. Whether you're able to take a full 24-hour day for rest or not, it may be helpful to move in that direction.

Take small and growing steps of faith into new areas, and you will see God bless and grow your work for his glory!

Questions to Ask in Pursuit of Vocational Wellness

- If my work is unsatisfying, is that because it doesn't suit me, or because of unhealthy relationships and interpersonal dynamics in my workplace? What do I have control over that I can change?
- Who has God made me to be, and how is he calling me to serve in the world?
- Who is God calling me to serve? (Consider your family, your faith community, the community where you live.)
- Where do I see an intersection between my skills, my passions, and the needs in the world around me?

Vocational Wellness Case Study

As Tamar's youngest child started high school, she felt ready to reenter the work force. Over the years while she stayed at home raising her children, she had kept up her bookkeeping skills and certifications by picking up occasional part-time and temporary side jobs. She enjoyed the challenges of helping small business owners organize their financial records and find places where they could optimize their spending. But she saw the future of AI and banking merging together in a way that she realized would eliminate needs for work like hers on a large scale. With a goal of making some money to be able to follow her dreams of traveling once the kids finally established their own lives, Tamar knew that starting a bookkeeping business of her own was out of the question.

As she considered her future, Tamar prayed and asked her Bible Study group to pray with her. She felt certain that God had a place for her where she could put her skills to use, make a difference, and be rewarded with a decent income. While she didn't see anything that suited her as she began to scour the job websites, she trusted that God had the right job for her at the right time.

One Tuesday morning, Christela came into their Bible Study bubbling with excitement. Her son and daughter-in-law had decided to start a nonprofit organization to serve low-income children in their city. They had built partnerships with local schools to identify families who could benefit from school supplies, meals on days when school was out, and other resources, and they had a host of local churches lined up to provide donations. While they had a fantastic vision and a lot of energy to make it happen, they lacked the ability to organize and manage the finances. They needed someone to help them with the final paperwork for their 501(c)3, apply for grants, keep track of financial donations, and generally run the business side. And Christela knew just the person to ask! Within a few months, Tamar had found work that suited her perfectly. Moreover, she took great delight in knowing that her skills were helping grow an important ministry to families in her community.

One key to Tamar's story is that she didn't rush in to find just any job but instead chose to wait for God to show her where he intended for her to use her skills. Through prayer and Connections with others, she found rewarding work. She discovered a vocation that allowed her skills to support work she enjoyed doing and felt passionate about.

Financial Wellness

Aiden found himself struggling financially. Rent was going up. He had lost a week of work due to illness, and with no sick pay, he lost a week of pay. He found a new job that paid better and provided full benefits, but it would be two weeks before he got his first check. And nagging at him underneath all of this was a load of credit card debt that had piled up from impulse purchases due to his unmanaged ADHD. He felt utterly defeated. Yet he found hope of getting out of his bind as he became aware of the root issues under his financial troubles and began to address them.

Aiden's story is relevant here because it demonstrates how Financial Wellness is more than a matter of income and expenses or a simple issue of spending. Physical and mental troubles as well as circumstances completely out of his control (the cost of housing, benefits offered by his employer and a delay in getting paid as he transitioned to a new job) had all played into his financial struggles.

Paul wrote in 1 Timothy 6:17, "Instruct those who are rich in this present world not to be conceited or to fix their hope on the uncertainty of riches, but on God, who richly supplies us with all things to enjoy" (NASB). This verse offers some significant perspective about finances. First, riches and wealth are uncertain. Lizzy and her husband experienced this. They were extremely diligent about managing their finances according to principles taught by Dave Ramsey through Financial Peace University, but when they both faced serious health problems, their financial stability evaporated. In December, 2021, our local community watched as nearly 1,000 families lost their homes to the Marshall Fire outside of Boulder, CO—and most of those families later discovered their insurance policies were inadequate to cover rebuilding their homes, leaving them in a huge financial bind. Because financial stability can be uncertain, Paul encouraged God's people to remember that only God is eternally secure. At the same time, Paul reminds us that God supplies us with things we can enjoy. These may be financial and material blessings, but God's blessings are not always defined by material abundance. Life is filled with beauty and many things to enjoy.

We like to look at Financial Wellness like the proverbial "canary in a coal mine." When things are out of balance or out of control financially, you might step back and look at other areas of your life. Are you working and serving in a way that uses your gifts and skills to the fullest? Are you stressed and spending money on things that you hope will help you feel better? If you're struggling to make a business succeed, is there an unhealthy belief underlying your struggles? Is something else out of balance? Could your finances be an indication that you are struggling to trust God in this or another area?

This is not to say that financial stability is an indication that everything else in your life is good. Perhaps it is, but our point here is that financial struggles may be an indication of being in "survival mode" rather than Thriving in other areas.

Principles of Financial Wellness

Earthly wealth is meant for providing for your household and delighting in God's provision.

Many places in the scriptures show us that God blesses us financially both to meet our everyday needs and to allow us to enjoy abundance when he gives it. God does not intend for us to store up or hoard our wealth for the sake of having more. (See the parable of the rich man in Luke 12:16-21.) Rather, God instructs his people to use their abundance to enjoy good things and to celebrate in his presence (Isaiah 55:2, Deuteronomy 14:26). Jesus said, "Do not store up for yourselves treasures on earth, where moths and vermin destroy, and where thieves break in and steal. But store up for yourselves treasures in heaven, where moths and vermin do not destroy, and where thieves do not break in and steal. For where your treasure is, there your heart will be also" (Matthew 6:19-21). If you store up or hoard anything, it is to be what lasts eternally, such as your relationship with God and others. This is not to say that saving for the future is outside of God's will. You can be wise and prepared while also continuing in an attitude of trust and delight in what God gives you today.

We give cheerfully, whether sacrificially or out of abundance, particularly to help those in need.

From the time God established the Hebrew people as a nation at the Exodus, he has asked his people to give for two primary purposes. First, God asks his people to support his work, whether it be the building of the tabernacle or the support of others working in ministry. Second, God asks us to provide for the needs of others. He condemns those who turn their backs on the poor. (See Malachi 2:17-3:5.)

Furthermore, we want to address the idea of "sacrificial giving" that has been elevated in the modern church's teachings. God encourages us to give out of our abundance and not necessarily to the point of hardship (see 2 Corinthians 8:13-15). The most important principle of giving is found in 2 Cor 9:7, "Each of you should give what you have decided in your heart to give, not reluctantly or under compulsion, for God loves a cheerful giver." Cheerful, purposeful giving is a sign of trust in God, and that pleases him greatly. When you give to support God's work and give to help people in need, your giving will be in line with his purposes.

Transformation happens when we focus our hopes on God, his work and provision, rather than on money and what it can provide.

With an awareness that God calls us to store up "heavenly treasures" and that cheerful, purposeful giving pleases him more than grudging sacrifice, we begin to see that what matters to him is not our bank accounts but our hearts. The verse we looked at from 1 Timothy is written to teach those who have wealth to keep their focus and hope in God rather than in their financial stability, but the converse is also true. Whether you have abundance or you struggle with a lack of finances, you will only find peace by keeping your hopes fixed on God. Trust him to provide for your needs and watch for evidence that he is at work. This is what God desires most of all: for his children to trust him to provide for their needs and to praise and rejoice in him in their abundance.

Using Financial Pain to Identify Areas of Need

As we noted earlier, financial struggles may point to an underlying core issue. Rarely is financial need simply an issue of insufficient income. Without discounting the reality of poverty, we have noticed people living from paycheck to paycheck at many income levels. If you're struggling, begin by taking an honest look at your income and expenses. Look at where your spending might be out of balance— eating out (or ordering from restaurants) often, indulging kids' demands for random things at the grocery store, heavy spending on personal items or other things. Are these symptoms of seeking to find comfort or avoid conflict because it's "easier" to spend money than to say no? Or are you refusing to accept assistance that you actually need? Examine why you don't want to ask for or accept help, even temporarily. As you choose to trust God and grow in this area, understand that he might have an unexpected lesson for you through this pain.

Practical Suggestions

Spending Tracker

The most powerful tool for Curiosity and awareness in this area is taking the time to look at how you spend your money. Keep a notebook with you for a month or two and write down every expense. As in all things, don't judge yourself, just notice. You don't have to track every penny, but it might help to write down approximate dollar amounts. Just be honest with yourself—no one else needs to see this, and if you "cheat" on your tracking, you won't gain much benefit. After several weeks, look for patterns in your spending. What do you notice? What can you choose to adjust in your spending?

Budget

Rather than looking at a budget as a spending constraint, you can view it as a tool to help you mindfully plan and manage your income. When you plan a budget, start with the nonnegotiables such as housing, car payments, food, and other regular bills. (If you don't know how much to budget for things like food or personal care, then go back and track your spending for a month before working on the budget.) Then add in more discretionary items—clothes, eating out, entertainment. Leave space in your budget for things you enjoy, even if it's only a small monthly indulgence. And as much as possible, set aside some money for savings so that you're prepared for both unexpected events as well as future needs.

Questions to Ask in Pursuit of Financial Wellness

- Am I wholeheartedly trusting God with my finances and financial stability?
- What beliefs do I have about money and finances?
- Have I made a purposeful plan for giving? If not, can I make a plan even for a small donation on a regular basis as an act of trust in God?
- If I am struggling in this area, could it be a symptom of another area where my life is not in line with God's plan for me? How can I make a simple change in this area to grow closer to what God is asking of me?

Financial Wellness Case Study

Alex had been raised in a family that faithfully practiced giving. While her parents didn't make a big deal about it, they did make a point of teaching their children to value giving. From the earliest age when she received an allowance, Alex had been taught to set aside part for savings, give part of the money to church, and then use the rest to spend on her needs and wants. It worked well in elementary and middle school. Later in high school, she fell out of the habit of giving regularly, even when she had a part-time job. Now as she approached the end of her graduate degree in biomechanical engineering, she weighed her school debt compared to her income prospects and mentally ruled out the prospect of giving away any of her money at this stage of her life. Maybe once she had been working a few years and paid down the debt a bit it would be practical, but definitely not now.

And then her little brother called. As he was about to graduate from college, he felt a call to go to the mission field. He had always been a steady, non-impulsive person, so she knew he had carefully thought out this decision and was following God to work in Guatemala. He asked her to consider giving towards his monthly need of $4000. How could she say no? But how could she say yes? Her finances felt out of control, and she worried about paying off her student loans. Still, she agreed to find $100 each month to give to this really important work.

Her university's Career Center offered financial counseling. Before making this commitment, Alex didn't believe she needed help. She would just get a job, make some money, keep doing what she had always been doing, and pay off the debt. Now she looked at her bank accounts, knowing she could barely make it from one paycheck to the next with more than $100 left, and wondered how she'd be able to scrape together enough money to help her brother. She swallowed her pride and made an appointment with a financial counselor. The counselor helped her understand her spending and uncover places where she could cut back. She agreed that she didn't really need to spend $6 twice a day for coffee. She began to change her shopping habits. Instead of going to the mall for "retail therapy" stress relief, she started taking a fitness class at the local gym, finding that it cost far less than she was spending on sweaters and boots that she rarely wore. When she landed her dream job, making pretty much what she had expected, she was able to set and stick to a budget. Before long, she found she could easily make the monthly donation to support her brother, and she increased it after six months.

Alex's story demonstrates how important awareness is to Financial Wellness. Before her brother asked for support for his calling to missions, she had no motivation to keep her finances organized or her spending under control. She valued giving, having been raised to do so by her parents, but more immediate desires (shopping) and needs (school loan debt) led her to believe that she couldn't give. When she did find ways to control her spending and live with a budget, she discovered a great deal of joy in being able to support her brother financially. Another key to her financial freedom was discovering that she was using shopping for stress relief. She just needed to make a simple change to how she managed her stress in order to live in greater Financial Wellness.

Part Three

Applying the Grace Cycle to Life

We hope that, as you read through the second part of this book, you identified one area where God is calling you to live more in alignment with his purpose for you. Now it's time to put it into practice through Acceptance and choosing to make One Simple Change at a time. In this final part, we hope to encourage you as you move into new habits in your life. As I often tell my children (and myself) when taking on something new, "It isn't easy, but it's worth it." God's Grace empowers you to become more like Jesus and to become the person he intends for you to be. And you need to begin to do things differently than you have always done. Like the crippled man at the Pool of Bethesda, stop trying to do what you've always done and instead follow the Holy Spirit's leading into new life. Remember you are not alone—lean on others to support you, encourage you, and hold you accountable as necessary. And Celebrate any and all progress in this area!

CHAPTER 7

Learning to Drive

"Therefore everyone who hears these words of
mine and puts them into practice is like a wise
man who built his house on the rock."

Matthew 7:24

It has probably been a good few years (maybe even decades) since you learned to drive, but we see this as a great metaphor for how to bring all of this together. No one learns to drive by mastering one skill at a time. You don't start with learning to turn the car on and off, then master the gas and brake pedals, followed by making a turn and then backing up. All of these skills need to be learned at the same time, if slowly. Yes, a new driver does well to begin practicing in a large open parking lot or other safe environment. But soon he learns to drive on the roads, then later in heavier traffic and at night.

When I was a new driver living outside of Baltimore, I absolutely refused to drive in the city, even with my parents in the car to help me be aware of the surroundings. I wasn't exactly terrified to drive in the city, but I felt uncomfortable with all the traffic, pedestrians, stoplights, and unpredictability of driving downtown. Out of the blue, one day when I was in college (still less than five years after getting my license), a friend needed a ride into the city to catch a bus to visit her boyfriend. I didn't hesitate when I offered to drive her. I'm sure when my parents heard about that, they must have rolled their eyes and said to themselves, "We knew she could do it!" (Fortunately, they didn't let on to me how they felt about it.) But at that point, I had been driving for long enough to feel confident not only driving in the downtown environment but also navigating my way there and back (in the days long before GPS navigation).

In the same way, you might be feeling a little overwhelmed with navigating these seven areas of Wellness in your life. Where do you start? All of these areas of your life interact with and impact one another. It is a well-known fact that physical exercise improves mental health, which can improve relationships and emotional health. But it might also take a change in mindset (a mental change) to prepare to make necessary physical, vocational, or relationship changes.

So do you start with everything all at once? Well, that seems overwhelming, doesn't it? Going back to our initial principles of Curiosity, Connection and Grace, you can begin by looking within and praying about where the deepest root of struggle is for you. Remember that you need Connection to God and yourself. This can look like prayerful introspection to become aware of a foundational change that will help you begin to make changes in your life. A new driver might need to learn focus and awareness of their surroundings before they're ready to get behind the wheel. Or they may have great focus and awareness but need to understand the mechanics of how to operate the vehicle. Or maybe they need to build confidence. In the same way, you need to look inside to determine what is the most important first step for you.

Take time to be still in God's presence and reflect on what is at the deepest level of your need for change. Don't rush this, but don't spend so much time in reflection that you don't do anything. If you're caught overthinking this, maybe that's a clue about where you need to begin. Perhaps it's an issue in your Mental Wellness such as perfectionism, or it might be a Spiritual issue around your trust in God or yourself. If you identify a few areas where God is leading you towards change, just choose one and don't stress over the others. Remember that you'll cycle back around eventually to work on something else.

Once you've identified a root issue, pause to explore, acknowledge, and Accept how this became a limiting issue in your life. Then consider what One Simple Change you can make in your life. For example, perhaps you identified a need to slow down and be aware of what's going on in your thoughts throughout your day. Your One Simple Change might be to take a few minutes every morning or evening to reflect and journal about what you experienced in the previous 24 hours, what emotions arose, and how you responded or reacted. Or perhaps you're aware that your body feels sluggish because you're not active, so you might look for a way to incorporate some movement into your days, whether it's a short walk after dinner, an exercise class at a local gym or recreation center, or trying a new exercise format that you haven't tried before. Some other examples of simple changes include the following: tracking your spending, Scripture meditation, a daily gratitude practice, or setting a bedtime alarm.

It can be challenging to incorporate a new habit in your life at times. I find that I might be good with a new habit for a few days or a week, but then I forget and fall out of the habit. The concept of "habit stacking" may be helpful. This is a simple way of adding a new habit onto an existing one.[37] There was a time when I was eating a vegetarian diet, and I discovered that I needed to supplement it with some nutrients. Unfortunately, I couldn't remember to actually take my vitamins every day. After a while, I would feel run down and realize that I needed to start taking the supplements again, but soon I would fall out of the habit. I tried leaving the bottles of vitamins on the kitchen table where I eat breakfast, but inevitably when Michael cleaned off the table, he put them away in the cabinet where I couldn't see them! (Yes, I could ask him not to put them away, but when we had guests over, I didn't want them sitting out anyway.) So I decided to pair taking my vitamins with a habit that I know I do consistently twice a day: brushing my teeth. I put the bottles by my bathroom sink and started taking them every morning and evening after brushing. Habit stacking is a simple way of using an existing habit to trigger a new one. Maybe doing the dishes after dinner is a reminder to step outside and go for a walk afterwards. You could adjust your bedtime routine to include five extra minutes of thinking back on your day and jotting down a few notes about what you experienced and how you showed up. (Remember that journaling does not need to take many paragraphs or pages!) Brewing your morning coffee or tea might give you a moment to look at your calendar for the day and set a reminder

---

37: For more on creating new habits, we recommend Clear, James. *Atomic Habits: An Easy & Proven Way to Build Good Habits & Break Bad Ones: Tiny Changes*, Remarkable Results. Cornerstone Press, 2022.

to call a friend, take a few minutes to go outside and enjoy nature, or simply stop what you're doing and breathe.

Over time, creating One Simple Change at a time will lead to larger changes in your life. Just as the new driver finds that looking at the road ahead helps her steer accurately and stay in the center of her lane—or that he can maintain a safe speed by being aware of other vehicles and his surroundings on the road rather than staring at the speedometer—you'll find that each simple, small change you make will impact other areas of your life. A daily gratitude or Scripture meditation practice might help you resolve some emotional or mental blocks in your life. Regular exercise of any kind is beneficial to your whole self, not just your physical body. Making progress towards Vocational or Financial Wellness is progress toward greater stability in other areas.

Start and continue this process with Curiosity and Connection. Return often to an awareness of how your new habit is working out, and if necessary try something different (such as the way I decided to put my vitamins by the bathroom sink instead of the kitchen table). Maybe you need to find a different exercise because you chose something that is too hard on your body or not challenging enough. You might find that a nutrition change you tried doesn't work successfully. If the simple change you choose doesn't lead to the progress you expect, it's okay. Reframe your thinking from "success or failure" to "progress or learning." There are no failures when you're seeking to live aligned with what God says is Good! Instead, something that doesn't work out teaches you more about yourself.

Remain in that place of Connection and nonjudgmental awareness with your body, mind, emotions, and spirit as you make changes. At the same time, stay connected with your supportive community, the people who are cheering you on and supporting you with accountability. When you choose to make a simple habit change, share that with others and give them permission to check on you. Through all of this, stay in God's presence, talking with him about how you feel and what is happening. Remember that God made you—every part of you—and he can help with insights into your self!

Never forget that you are empowered by God's Grace. As you choose to make changes, by God's Grace, believe that you can. He promises in Philippians 1:6 that he will complete the good works he begins in you. Since you are choosing transformation led by him, trust and lean on him. Celebrate your progress along the way—not waiting until you fully achieve a goal, but acknowledging every small step towards growth.

"His divine power has given us everything we need for a godly life through our knowledge of him who called us by his own glory and goodness" (2 Peter 1:3). You have everything you need through the power of God's Grace. The "godly life" Peter refers to here is simply a life that is led by God and lines up with what his word says is Good. Before you know it, you'll be navigating your way through something as challenging as driving in downtown Baltimore once felt to me. You'll realize with gratitude that you were able to do something you never imagined possible!

CHAPTER 8

Beyond Self-Care

"Pay attention to the welfare of your innermost
being, for from there flows the wellspring of life."

Proverbs 4:23 TPT

In a sense, this whole book has been about self-care. Our aim has been to help you identify areas where your body, spirit, heart, and mind need restoration and to give you a framework for moving closer to God and living in Grace. When you're able to live in this way, you'll experience peace and lasting joy in your life. This peace will help you to live in strength and balance. Sadly, many of us experience a life filled with expectations and demands from others and from ourselves. We run ourselves to stress and overwhelm before we realize we need a break. Our hearts and souls become depleted. We need restoration.

That is the point of self-care: to restore your heart, mind, spirit, and body so that you can continue living in service to God and others.

What does this look like? You might be wondering if I'm talking about a night out with friends, getting massages or pedicures, working out at the gym, eating nourishing foods... or something else. The answer is that self-care for you is what you need to refresh and restore yourself. We might think of "self-care" activities on a continuum. At one end we'd put basic activities of survival and hygiene (bathing, brushing teeth, eating). At the other end we put pampering activities. Pampering looks different for everyone. In the middle we might have health and wellness activities: preventive health exams and exercise, for example. Then a little further on, we might move into activities that feed our minds: education (not just primary or secondary education but also learning new things throughout life). From there, we can add activities that restore our hearts, souls, and minds: creative pursuits, travel, appreciation of music and art.

Self-Care Continuum

| basic hygiene | health care | exercise | education | creative & restorative | pampering |

As I name some of these activities, I'm aware that you might put different activities in different places on this continuum than I would. For some, getting a pedicure is an unnecessary pampering indulgence, while for others it's considered a necessity for hygiene. Regular massages may be part of what one person needs for maintaining general health, but for others, a massage is a pampering indulgence. Travel might be a luxury or a need for you. As you look at this diagram, name the activities that you would put in each place. Build your own self-care continuum, recognizing that this is unique to you.

Is it okay to indulge and pamper yourself as part of your self-care? Remember that we said earlier that God intends us to use the finances he provides for enjoyment. If you are able to indulge in some pampering activities, then do so with gratitude to God for his provision!

We see examples of people practicing self-care in a few places in the Bible. Jesus took time away from the crowds and even from his disciples because he needed restoration. He spent time alone with his Father. He also took time in community with his close inner circle of disciples and friends. In Jesus's example, we see a new paradigm for self-care, something that we like to call "Mutual Care."

Mutual Care is being restored in the presence of and spending time with others with whom we have loving relationships. This includes God. While we advocate practicing this as much as possible, we recognize that it is an ideal but not always practical. Sometimes when I seek to spend time alone with God, I am interrupted by a child who wants to be with me. You may not have a spouse or close friend who is always available when you need restoration. However, we encourage you to cultivate your relationships with God and others to a place where you can find restoration in their presence. You'll find that this becomes truly mutual, a back-and-forth refilling of each other's empty places. Even more, being in a close relationship with someone who knows you well provides additional depth. Having a person in your life who can look at you and say, "You look depleted. How can

I support you? What do you need?" is a tremendous blessing, as is the beauty of being able to offer that kind of support to another person.

As you practice self-care for restoration, also work on building relationships with others that can move towards Mutual Care. Many mental health professionals are beginning to recognize that "self-care, in its current form has pulled us away from one another, encouraging solitude over connection."[38] Isolated self-care practices may be contributing to increasing loneliness in our world. Looking at your own self-care continuum, at what point or points could it be helpful or important for you to invite others in to join you? Some people need others to support them in basic activities, while others look at this spectrum and would think, "I've got this all on my own!" Yet God never meant for anyone to live in isolation. We need God and others, and we need to invite others into our own care as well. This might look like reaching out to a friend to go to an art class together, joining a group fitness class, or finding a companion for a trip somewhere.

Let's take a moment to consider "alone time." Quiet, silence, and time alone are essential to our well-being. Sometimes it's impossible to think clearly without being alone, and sometimes you need a break from all the noise and chaos that surrounds you. Yet are you ever truly alone? God is always present with you, so recognize that time "alone" is truly time in his presence. With that in mind, ask and allow God to restore you when you're alone with him.

God created us with important needs in all areas of our lives: physical, spiritual, mental, emotional, relational, vocational, and financial. You might seek to meet all of these needs on your own, but

38: Volpe, Allie. "How the Self-Care Industry Made Us so Lonely." *Vox*, 3 June 2024, www.vox.com/even-better/350424/self-care-isolation-loneliness-epidemic.

why would you if you can do so in Connection with God and others? Rather than following a typical pattern of pouring out from yourself to others until you're depleted, then going it alone to find restoration, we encourage you to be aware of God resourcing and filling you, both when you are "on the go" and when you are alone. Invite others to join you on this journey, others who are seeking to grow in the same direction and with the same understanding of what God says is Good. Engage in relationships where you are mutually building one another up. And remember that you are resourced and able to grow and experience this transformation by Grace!

CHAPTER 9

Shalom

"You will keep in perfect peace those whose
minds are steadfast because they trust in you."

Isaiah 26:3

We all crave a life of peace, stability, confidence.

A life characterized by *Shalom*.

When we speak of *Shalom*, a Hebrew word frequently translated as "peace," we mean far more than calm or rest from our troubles. *Shalom* carries a complex meaning that includes peace, prosperity/success, health/well-being, friendliness, and salvation or deliverance from troubles.[39] This is a life of complete Wellness, what we like to call Wholeness. In our bodies, spirits, minds, and hearts we seek to Thrive

---

39: "Word Info: in Perfect Peace," Logos: Deep Bible Study app version 28.0.4, Faithlife Corporation, Logos Bible Software, www.logos.com.

in *Shalom* Wholeness as God intends for us. In our relationships, work, and finances, we long to enter and engage with the world from this place of perfect peace. We long to live out of this place of peace and presence to God and others so that we can bring light and love to others.

Shalom Wholeness often grows out of walking with God through very hard circumstances, even suffering. Michael and I have both individually and as a couple experienced seasons of intense struggle that have led us to a new experience of quiet confidence and trust in God's love and goodness. From that confidence, we have learned to live in greater stability despite the storms of life.

Perhaps you've touched this sense of *Shalom* at times in your life. Or maybe you look at others you know and think, "If they can live in peace, I should be able to also!" Each person has a very unique, individual journey through life. We encourage you to release any self-judgment or expectations for yourself that come with the word "should." Sadly, most of the church's teachings have led us all to believe we need to strive, always working and doing activities that we believe will bring us closer to God. You may feel like you owe God something because he has saved you, so you live constantly trying to make him happy with you and your service. Friend, please rest from your striving. God loves you. Period. He is already happy—dare we say thrilled—with you exactly as you are! Rather than draining your life with constant work and service that leaves you exhausted (and possibly wondering how you're going to make it to the end of your life looking even remotely like a human), seek God. Seek relationship with him. Seek to know him, to know what is important to him. Seek to know the depth of his love for you.

Is there hope for living in *Shalom* Wholeness? Yes. God did not redeem us from our brokenness intending for us to stay in that state. He redeemed us so that we could grow to reflect his image through Christ. Your renewal can begin today, in this very moment, as you surrender to God and his love. Jesus said, "Come to me all you who are weary and burdened, and I will give you rest" (Matthew 11:28). Jesus made this offer right after he condemned the towns of Galilee where he had been ministering. They had not repented in response to the miracles he had done there. The people in these towns were not "bad"; they were very religious, working carefully and diligently to follow God's Law. When Jesus came to them, he sought to give them rest, peace, and hope, but they chose to remain busily occupied with their works. When we feel "weary and burdened" from our striving to do all the things we feel we should do to please God, Jesus invites us to come to him, to lay down our burdens, share the yoke he has for us, and experience true rest. He invites us into *Shalom*.

Consider how often Jesus told people they needed to come to him as little children: humble, not knowing everything, trusting and following him. He doesn't want you to come to him with your earthly wisdom, experiences, and expectations. When you lay these things down at his feet and come to him open for what he intends to give you, then you begin to experience true rest and peace. *Shalom* begins when you release your striving and the limits of your human experience and knowledge so that you can allow the Holy Spirit to fill these places with his presence. He replaces striving with peace, rest, and *Shalom* Wholeness.

It doesn't happen all at once. This is a process that goes on throughout the course of our lives. In his kindness, God makes us aware of one area (or maybe a few areas) of our lives that he desires to change, and then he begins working in that area. He doesn't push in to completely overhaul our lives all at once! With that in mind, keep in mind the hope of living in greater *Shalom* as a lifelong journey rather than an end goal. You will grow and learn and keep coming back to The Grace Cycle repeatedly, finding a deeper experience of Wholeness in life. Keep in mind that God is seeking your transformation because he sees the person he created and intended for you to be. You will grow more like Jesus and reflect God's image into the world, and you will discover inside of you true peace and joy that comes from living out of who you are meant to be.

You move closer to living in *Shalom* Wholeness by aligning your life with what God's Word says is Good. Use Curiosity to explore what works (or doesn't work) for you as a unique individual, remembering that what works for one person may or may not work for another who has a different body, mind, spirit, and life experiences. Remain in Connection with God, community, and your self throughout your life, living in awareness and seeking support for your transformation. Remember that God's Grace empowers you throughout it all. These three tools—Curiosity, Connection and Grace—intertwine and work together as you follow the Grace Cycle to Thrive in *Shalom* Wholeness.

As you finish this book, take some time to dive into Curiosity in your life. Identify one area where God is calling you to transformation leading to *Shalom* Wholeness. Who is your Community, your people who can support you in your journey? Seek out people who love you, who will tell you the truth and call you forward in your transformation without expressing judgment. Build new habits through Grace, relying on God to empower you and complete the work he has begun (Philippians 1:6). If you need additional support, Karen runs a program with both individual and group coaching support. We would love to hear from you at karen@1fit.us to explore whether we can help you in your journey of transformation.

Just before his arrest and crucifixion, Jesus said to his disciples, "Peace I leave with you, my peace I give you. I do not give to you as the world gives. Do not let your hearts be troubled and do not be afraid" (John 14:27). He knew that his closest friends were about to enter into a terrifying few days, watching his physical life end and beginning to live without having him present to teach them and show them what to do. He said this immediately after promising that the Father would send the Holy Spirit to teach and guide them in his physical absence. He promised his *Shalom* peacefully, completely, and permanently. We encourage you to accept this promise for yourself. Following the Holy Spirit and the good direction laid out in the Bible, you can grow in a life of peace, health, rest, and Wholeness.

Abundant Blessings to you as you move forward in your journey towards *Shalom* Wholeness!

Gratitude

Decades ago, we jokingly invented a "Theology of Brownie Points." According to this "theology," any time we express thanks for a person, they get "Brownie Points" that they can trade in for brownies when they get to Heaven. And God makes the best brownies! So we'd like to give Brownie Points to a number of people.

We would not be who we are without our families. The memories, joys, and challenges of these relationships have shaped us. Thank you to our parents, John and Fran Hampton and David and Jane Dittman, for loving us and investing in our lives from the very beginning. Fran and Jane, while you have both left us, we know you have joined the "great cloud of witnesses" and are cheering us on from Heaven's bleacher seats. We are grateful for our siblings, Nancy, Johnny, Dave, Steven, and Duane, for living life with us for decades.

To our children and grandchildren, thank you for enduring all of our mistakes and accepting our love. We trust that, as we continue to seek growth, we will inspire you all to live the lives that God has set out for you.

Over the last several years, some specific people and ministries have helped us in our journey and influenced our thinking on the subject of the Christian life and living in Wholeness. These include:

- Bob Hudson and Sharon Potzer and their work in The Cross Ministries Group (Men at the Cross/Women at the Cross)
- Rabbi Gene Binder, Brian Carlucci, and Cornerstone Church of Boulder, CO
- Dr. John Mark Lamb who opened our eyes to a powerful understanding of attachment

To Linette Williams whose persistence and love helped Karen find a new path away from living in brokenness to a journey towards wholeness, and to all my sisters in the WATC community who continually inspire me to keep doing my work with hope.

To Matthew Boardwell, for your unfailing love and leadership of Life Song Church. You have been a shepherd to us and to many others, modeling the faithful love of God. Your friendship, even from a distance, has been especially encouraging and a blessing to Michael.

To our faith community at His Shelter Church, we are grateful for your honesty, for giving us opportunities to teach and lead, for supporting us in faithful prayer. Natasha and Marty, your love and trust has encouraged and empowered us far more than you know.

To Morgan Gist MacDonald, Brian Dooley, and the amazing team at Paper Raven Books. Morgan, you have built a top-notch team to support authors, and knowing you're a kindred spirit gave me confidence to work with you all. Brian, you may never realize how your belief in this work kept me going when I questioned sharing this message with the world.

Above all to God—Father, Son, and Holy Spirit—for love that we can never fathom, for inspiration to write this book, for drawing us always onward and upward.

Enhance Your Journey with a Free Printable Reflection Journal!

Thank you for reading *Thriving in Grace: Unleashing Wellness from a Biblical Perspective*. To deepen your study and application of the principles in this book, we're excited to offer you a free, printable reflection journal!

Visit our website to download your free journal and enrich your journey toward wellness with thought-provoking questions, insightful reflections, and practical exercises.

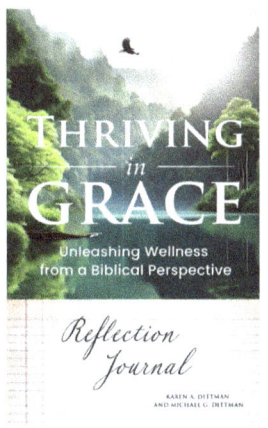

Dive deeper into the Scriptures and unleash wellness from
a Biblical perspective. Start your transformative journey today!

http://thrivingjournal.1fit-wellness.com

www.ingramcontent.com/pod-product-compliance
Lightning Source LLC
Chambersburg PA
CBHW071718140626
46557CB00012B/945